HOW TO DRAW PEOPLE

USING

EARLY COPY BOOKS

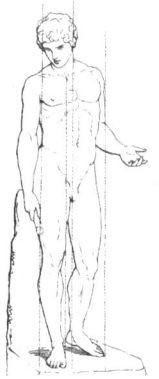

By Tom Richardson

Early Copy Books

Published by Tom Richardson
ISBN 978-0-9821678-8-5

HOW TO DRAW PEOPLE
USING
EARLY COPY BOOKS

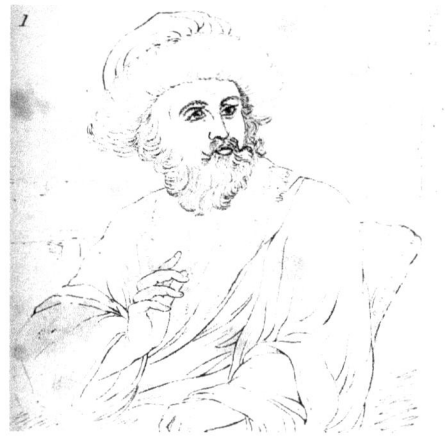

from Buchanan's Initiatory Drawing Lessons

Table of Contents

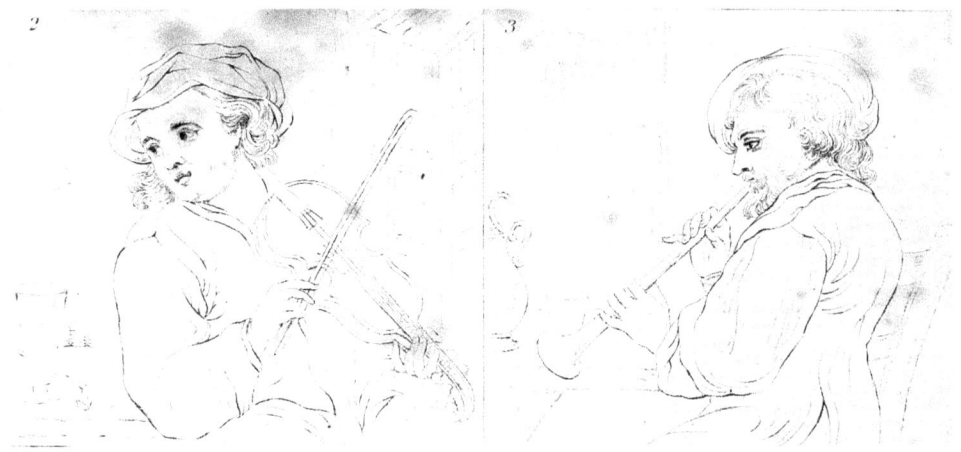

from Buchanan's Initiatory Drawing Lessons

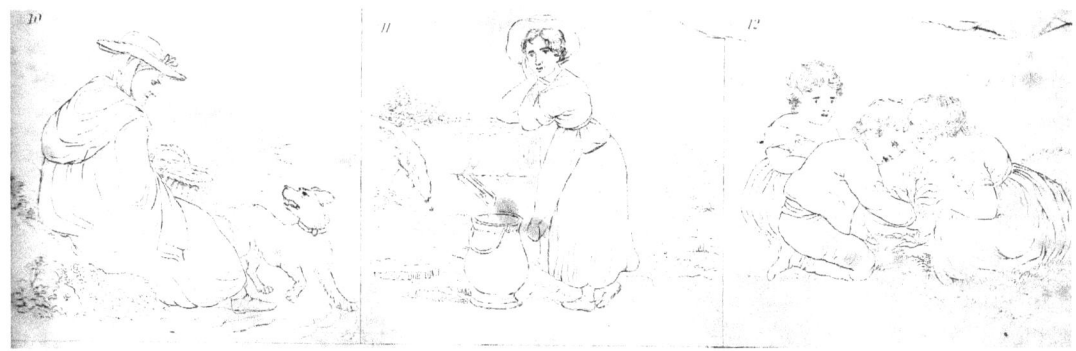

from Buchanan's Initiatory Drawing Lessons

INTRODUCTION

In the eighteenth century there was a great movement to teach drawing through the use of copy books. There was a philosophical opinion that acquiring skill in drawing would transfer both to other intellectual endeavors and to vocational success.

In the opinion of these teachers there was no better way to learn to draw than through copying the works of those who had mastered the art. Typically the student was encouraged to study am example of a master's work and then reproduce it freehand.

Most books approached the subject through a series of exercises beginning with drawing simple lines, then parallel lines, then simple shapes and learning to shade simple shapes, proceeding to more complex shapes and subsequently the human figure.

This book of reproductions of drawings from early copy books skips the initial steps and jumps right to the human figure.

John Chapman produced a massive and well known book of this type in 1858 in which he sets forth the basic premise:

"Anyone who can learn to write can learn to draw and, as writing is not taught to those only who are destined to become authors, but as forming an essential part of general education, so is drawing equally important to others besides professional artists. To write —to draw a form or figure that shall be recognized as the representative of a letter or word, is one tiling; and to be able to design, draw, or write such forms, upon principles of grace and accuracy—to understand the Art of writing — is another. Thus it is also with Drawing, another mode of expressing ourselves, not less useful or necessary than that by letters or words. To draw a horse, that shall not be mistaken for a man, is one step; but to draw a horse, with all his just proportions and developments, movement and expression, is an Art to be acquired. Any one can make something on paper to look like a tree, a cottage, a road, a brook, or a mountain; but Art goes farther, and, as if to compensate for what it falls short of, invests the whole with a charm more impressive than the reality, even to the most simple-minded cow-boy, who may have gone that road or waded that brook a thousand times, unconscious of the beauty that surrounded him, until it was developed by the hand of Art".

"Who has ever hesitated to teach a child to write, because it was not intended that he should be an author? How many regard the art of Drawing as being of no practical importance, as a branch of education, to any but professional artists; and consider it, in its most favorable light, as a mere accomplishment — a pursuit only for the man of leisure? The resources of our schools are often exhausted in "finishing" our youth with " every accomplishment;" laid on so lightly, that, for all real and practical purposes, they are as ephemeral as the gay tints of the painted butterfly. Smatterings of languages, living and dead, are heaped upon them, while the great, universal language, the language of Design, is forgotten; or only thought of in the production of some huge "castle and ruins, with a man and a boy with a stick; and a dog"—painted by the teacher, under the scholar's direction, to hang in the parlor, as the veritable, first, and last, and only production, of the latter: who at once assumes, therefrom, an oracular authority in all matters connected with the Fine Arts, and leaves admiring friends in wonder, at what "he might have done, had he not given it up." To such, it may be said, "You have never begun."

"It is not only as a beautiful accomplishment, or a source of amusement for leisure moments, that the art of Drawing should be cultivated. It has its practical uses, in every occupation of life. It opens to all inexhaustible sources of utility, as well as pleasure; practices the eye to observe, and the hand to record, the ever-varying beauty with which nature abounds, and spreads a charm around every object of God's beautiful creation, unfelt and unknown to those who have failed or neglected its cultivation. It does more: it gives strength to the arm of the mechanic, and taste and skill to the producer, not only of the embellishments, but actual necessities of life. From the anvil of the smith and the workbench of the joiner, to the manufacturer of the most costly productions of ornamental art, it is ever at hand with its powerful aid, in strengthening invention and execution, and qualifying the mind and hand to design and produce whatever the wants or the tastes of society may require."

This is a review of the first book Buchanan's Initiatory Drawing Lessons from The New Monthly Magazine, Literary Journal March 1, 1928:

Buchanan's Initiatory Drawing Lessons. 4to.. 21s. Glasgow.

We have already noticed these initiatory drawing lessons in the form of numbers. The idea is excellent, of teaching drawing, sufficient for all useful purposes, and writing at the same time. Mr. Buchanan hat recently published Lithographical Lessons for black-lead pencil, but these by no meant equal the former ones for the pen. This speedy mode of acquiring drawing la well worthy of introduction into all schools, where writing it taught to the lower. classes on the most economical principles, and might be adopted in charity and national schools with great effect. Indeed, country schoolmasters, particularly, would do well to procure this simple work, and to adopt the plan laid down in it, without delay.

The drawings vary in sophistication, but the advice is, in every case, sound and the modern student will find much to learn from these old books.

BUCHANAN'S INITIATORY DRAWING LESSONS
Published by R. Buchanan

The first book which is reproduced was published in Edinburgh, Scotland, United Kingdom at an address which within the area where the University of Edinburgh is located today. It is titled *Buchanan's Initiatory Drawing Lessons for the use of Writing Academies and Private Families - Engraved Series to be copied with the pen.*

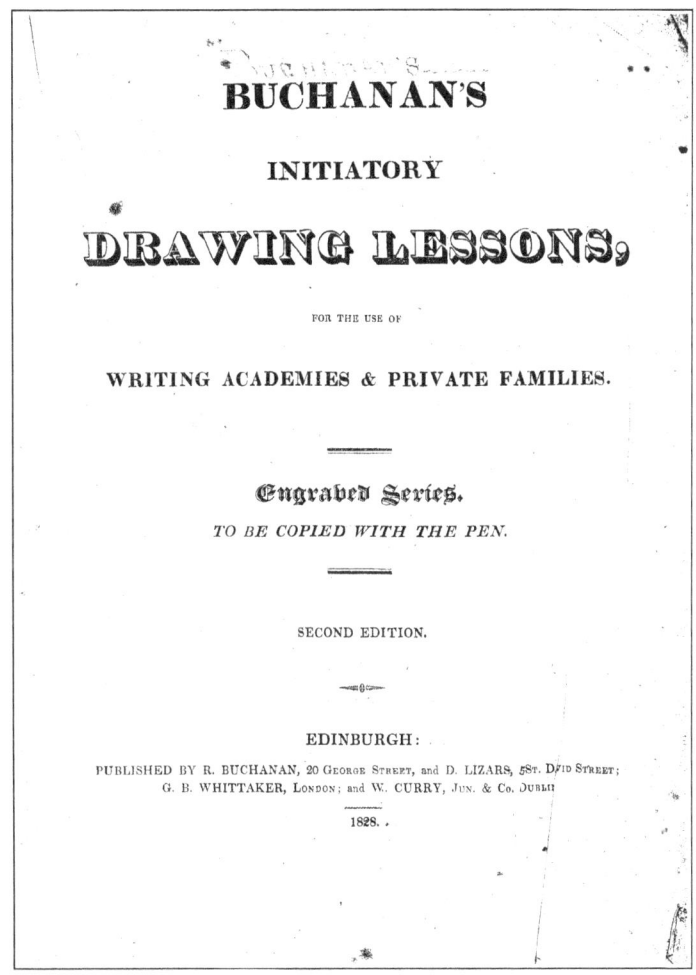

At the beginning of the book is an introduction titled "HINTS" which sets forth the common system of copying from the books and learning drawing through a sequential series of steps.

HINTS

Offered to the Notice of those who countenance the Teaching of Drawing according to the Plan followed by
BUCHANAN, GREENCOCK, AND R. BUCHANAN, EDINBURGH

1. Begin with the simplest Lessons in the series, and persevere in copying them, according to their order, onward to the most difficult, and do not indulge and fastidious desire to wander from the plan; as in most cases more will depend upon a systematic perseverance, than even upon what are called taste, genius, turn, &c.

2. If Introduced into a Public School, and taught without any addition to the usual fee, let one day of the week be allotted for the purpose, and let the Pupils suspend their Writing for that day, and employ it is Drawing. To teach it, however, an hour or two upon the Saturday forenoons, for a small addition to the quarter fee, has been found to answer fully better.

3. Provide a folio for holding paper, patterns, and a tin or brass case for pencils, &c.

4. Arrange the Pupils in classes, according to their merit, if it conveniently can be done.

5. Permit compasses to be used, if required. The Pupils will lay aside such helps when they can do without them.

6. Let the Pupils severally have their own sets of Lessons, and undeviatingly proceed in copying them in the order in which they are arranged. If this be not rigidly enforced, the Teacher will be so incessantly teased by capricious demands for this and that new pattern, that he will find his temper ruffled, and be robbed of his time by trying unsuccessfully to please the children, till they, in their turn, become so dissatisfied, that, to a certainty, they will ultimately give up the study in disgust.

7. Hurry and impatience are to be vigilantly guarded against, and slowness and neatness to be rigidly inculcated: if this be disregarded, there will be no proficiency, as the former are great faults to be avoided, and are commonly besetting evils to young Drawing Scholars. The usual plea of the task being too difficult must not be listened to, and the calls for assistance that will be made must be sparingly complied with: if they are often complied with, little good will be done; indeed the more help given by the Teacher, the less attention and labour will be bestowed by the Pupil. Plain and distinct directions, and the manner of working slightly exemplified upon their copies, will be in most cases sufficient.

8. After the outline is correctly made, and the sketch is to be gone over with the pen, run down Indian ink with water upon a saucer or plate, till it comes with such a consistency that it will give a black line, but no so thick as to prevent it flowing freely.

9. Beginners must be cautioned against making *continuous* lines, or of *sloping* them like writing, which they will naturally do; but let them be shewn how to do them, in a *broken*, *interrupted*, or *dotted* manner, especially in representations of ruins &c. , and afterwards to connect them in a free and spirited manner.

10. Imaginary, or even real black-lead lines, drawn through a pattern and the copy, will greatly assist the learned in attaining to correctness: for example, let a vertical line be drawn, or suppose it to be drawn in the pattern, and observe through which parts it passes; let a similar line be made, or supposed to be made, upon to Pupil's copy, and it will show similarity or dissimilarity in the copy. These lines may also be made horizontally, slantingly, or in any other direction.

11. Place beginners, who show carelessness or levity, beside scholars who go on more industriously and consider them as under their charge, and in some respects responsible for their promise.

12. Praise and blame may be used with effect, but they require to be managed with great delicacy and discretion.

13. Some Scholars, in numerous schools, who are more advanced, may be induced to give their assistance to the junior Scholars, if they are taught some separate branch by the Teacher, as a remuneration for their services.

14. The promise of a prize, such as a black-lead pencil, for a well-done component—a penknife for a

well-done page—a paint-box for a book well done, &c. without a blot, or a leaf wanting, will do much as encouragements.

15. If assistants are employed, they may call up to them the Pupils alternately, and work a little for each upon their pieces during the hour.

16. To make fine pictures is not so much the object in teaching from the sketches to be done with the pen and Indian ink, as to acquire a facility of representing objects by a free and correct outline, and which may be considered rather as useful than Ornamental Drawing.

17. Shading is but slightly introduced, and not so much with a view to produce effect, as to show where it should be. In the Lithographic Series, however, the Lessons are highly finished in the style of black-lead pencilings, and in copying the a hard kind of pencils ought to be used in outlining, and crayons of a softer kind for shading.

18. By attending to these hints, parents, or public or private Teachers, although they may not have previously studied Drawing, may undertake to teach it to others; and if they persevere, may acquire skill in it themselves, and render it, what it was in Athens, a common branch of elementary education.Should any who attempt it fail in not making their Pupils learn, it may be concluded that these hints have not been well attended to.

19. The minuteness of some of the Lessons has been captiously objected to, but as it is well known that even a microscopic exactness is required in some departments, such as Architecture, Mechanics, Natural History, &c., habits of close and scrupulous attention to minuteness must prove advantageous rather than hurtful to the Pupil afterwards.

20. If electors of Teachers for parish schools, and other elementary seminaries, were to make it a condition that the successful candidate should act upon the plan, it would rapidly spread among a class of people who could be most essentially benefited from its use; and were influential individuals, residing in the vicinity of such schools, to excite an honourable rivalry among the Students, by holding out little prizes of merit, such as a silver medal, with an appropriate inscription upon it, to the most deserving, it would call forth abilities which might prove highly useful to their possessor, and which, otherwise, might have remained uncultivated, and lost to the world.

21. As the plan can hardly be said to invade the province of the professed Drawing-Master, instead of creating alarm in the minds of such, it perhaps to the contrary, ought rather to be encouraged by them as a nursery for raising Pupils for them, whom they might, from time to time, transplant into their own classes.

from Buchanan's Initiatory Drawing Lessons

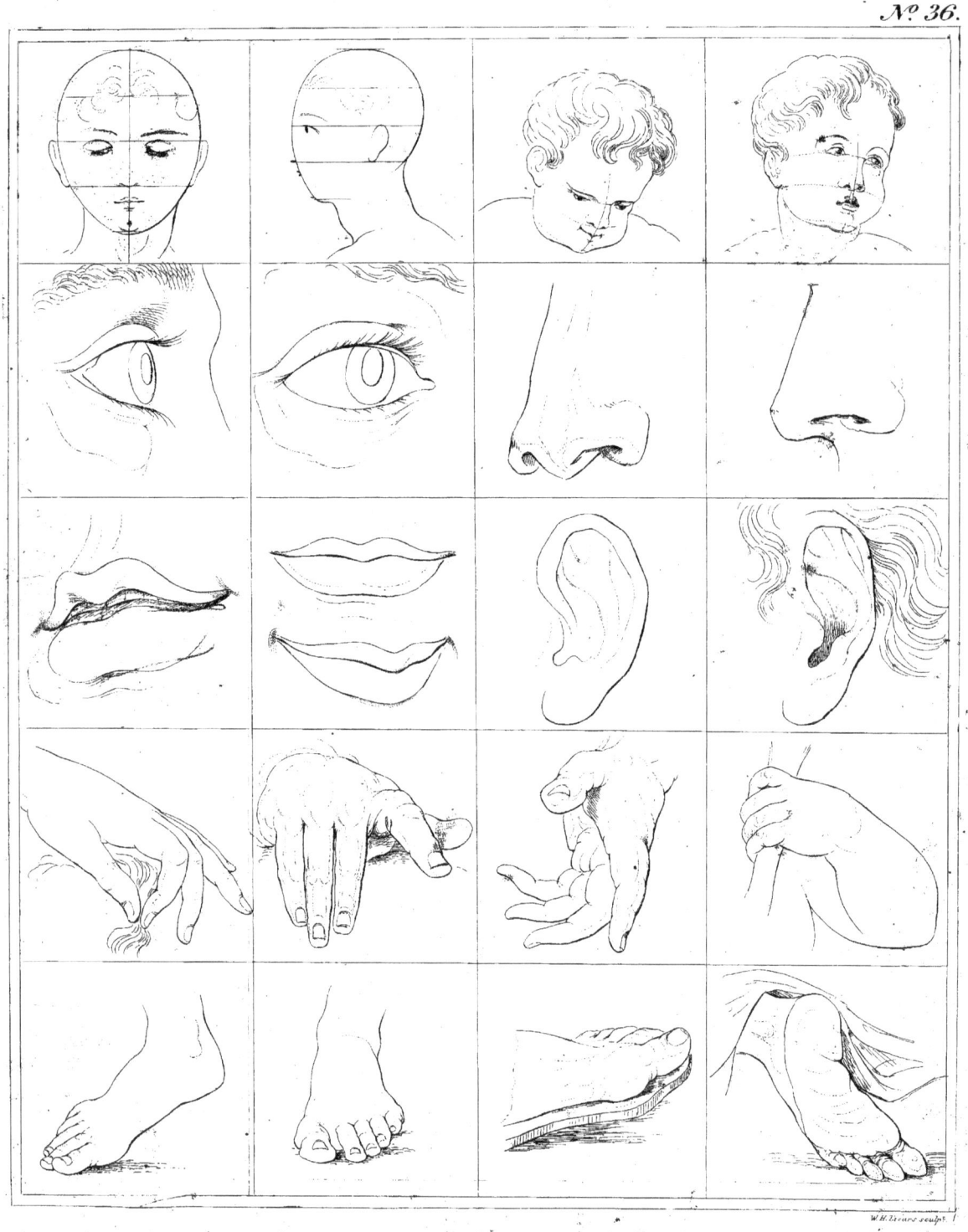

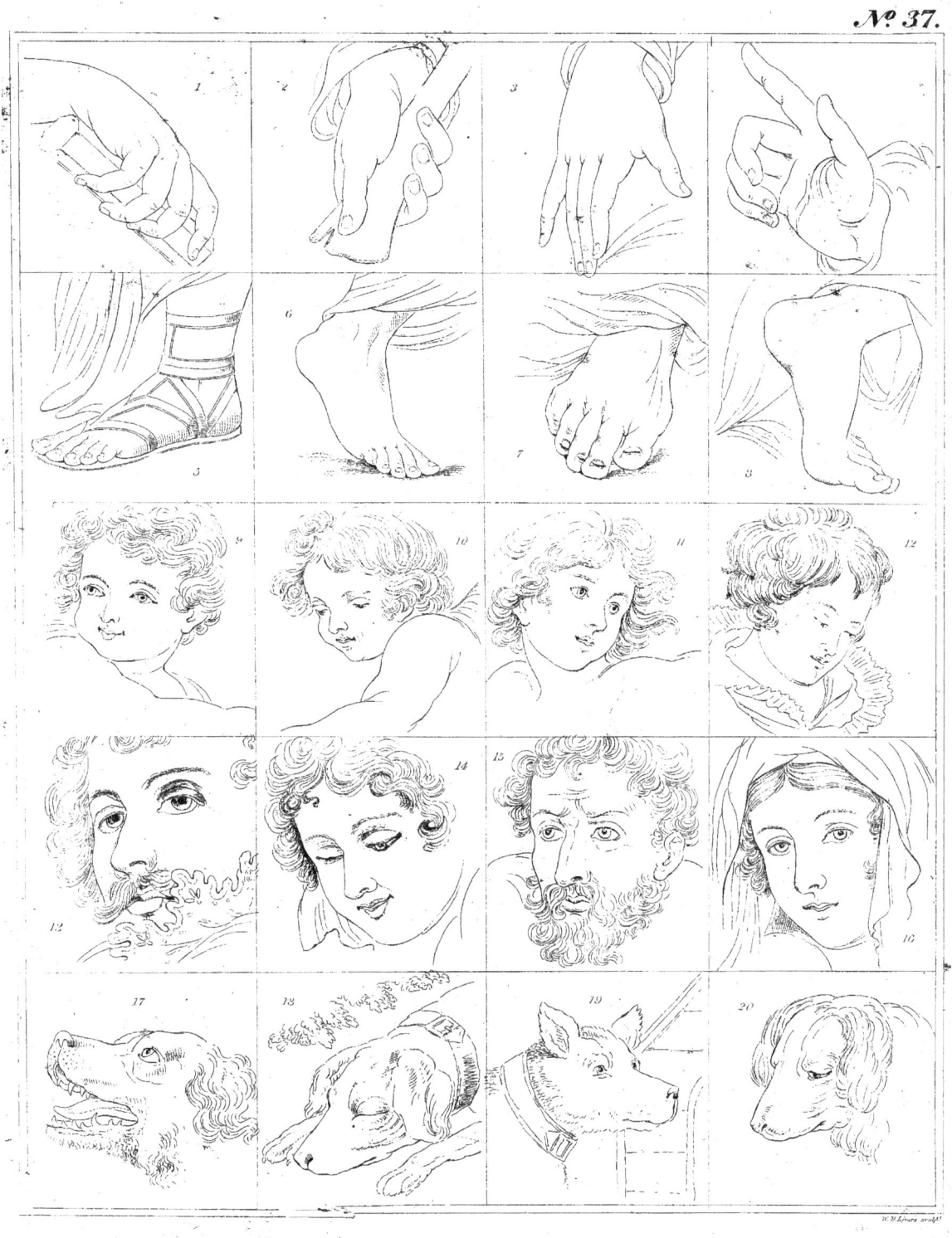

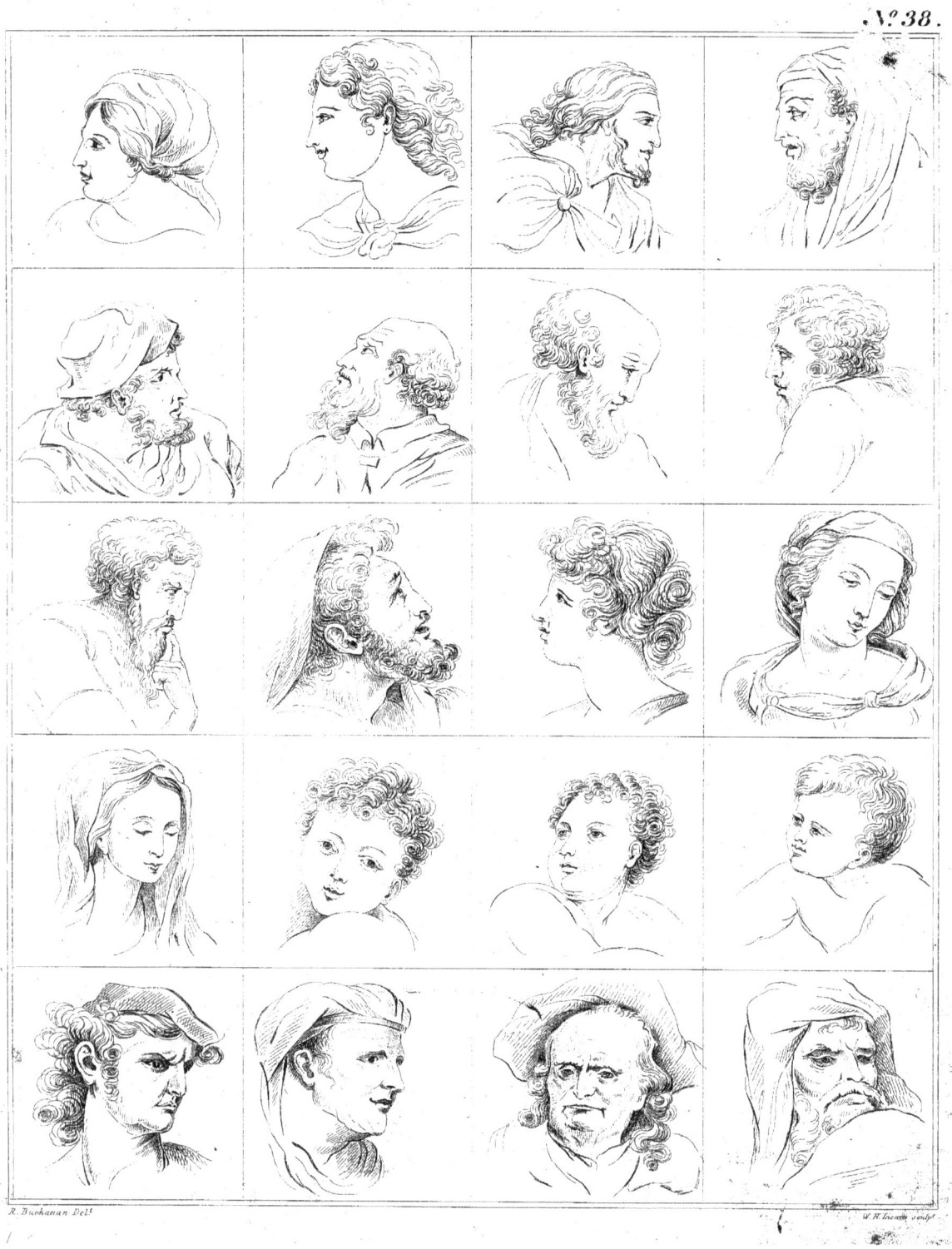

THE ILLUSTRATED DRAWING BOOK
By Robert Scott Burn

The next book is *The Illustrated Drawing – Book for the use of Schools, Students, and Artisans containing I. Pencil Drawing, II. Figure and Art, III. Perspective, &c., IV. Engraving with Three Hundred Illustrative Drawings and Diagrams* by Robert Scott Burn, published in London, England.

The introduction reinforces the practice of learning drawing in a step-by-step method of starting with simple shapes and proceeding to more complicated sketches.

"As all drawings are reducible to certain lines and figure, we hold it necessary to teach the student, in the first place, to draw these elementary parts with the utmost facility; following these, by a series of examples, from the simplest up to the most complicated sketch which may be offered to him; and them, by an advance to the more intricate riles, making plain the laws of vision (the foundation of perspective), so as to enable him to delineate correctly the various views in which these are exemplified. We require the student thoroughly to understand the reason why every operation is performed as directed, not merely to give him a facility for copying any determined object without reference to principles."

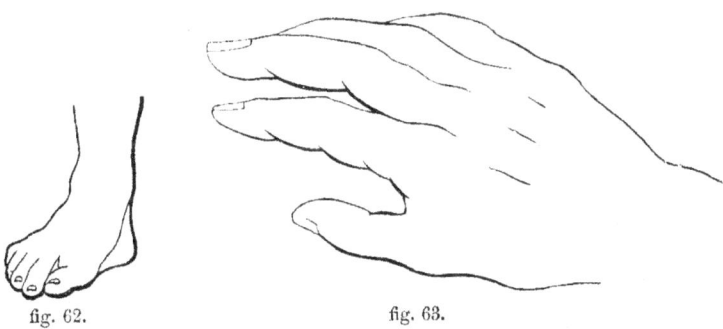

fig. 62.   fig. 63.

The sketch in fig. 62, representing a human foot, may be put in, by first drawing the general outline, thereafter finishing he details. Fig 63, 64, and 65 will be drawn in the same manner.

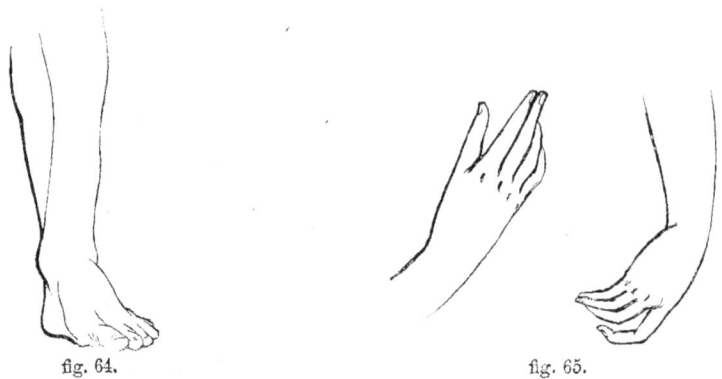

fig. 64.

fig. 65.

PROPORTIONS OF THE HUMAN FIGURE

We have deemed it best to treat from the other department, of the proportions which different parts of the human frame bear to each other, according to the acknowledged standard of beauty, as derived from measurements from the antique. We trust that the student will find the lessons here given of great assistance in enabling him to draw from casts. We should advise him to habituate himself to the practice, as it will lay a foundation for attaining with ease a correctness of proportion, which constitutes the chief beauty in drawing of the human figure. He must not, however suppose that beauty is always attained by attention to these rules, correctness being the principal point they have in view. There are many styles of beauty, the qualities of some consisting in a slight deviation in some point or other from the *established* proportions.

We first begin with the various parts of the human "head divine"—the seat of the soul, as some term it. The mouth, of which a sketch is given in fig. 1, is equal in width to the length of one eye and a half, and the height to one-half. The mouth in profile is exactly the same height, but only half the width; the upper lip projects less than the lower one. The nose in width is

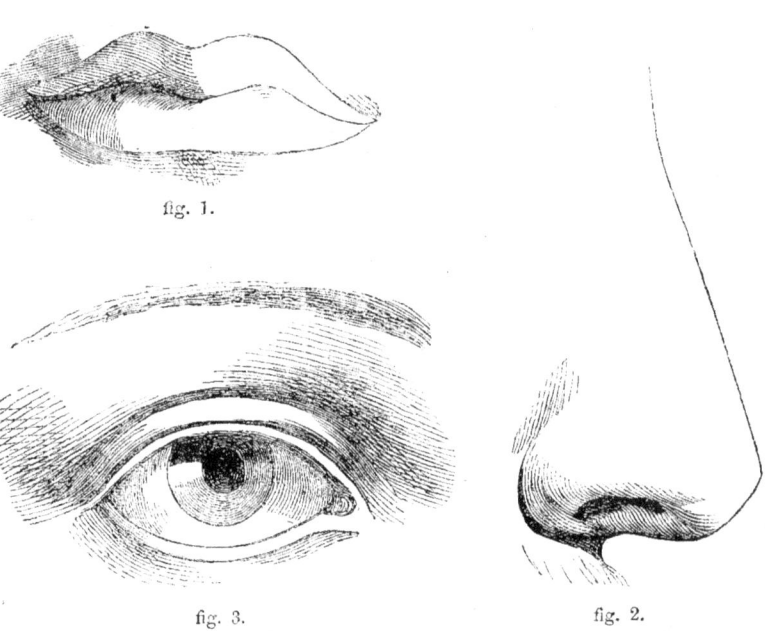

fig. 1.

fig. 3.

fig. 2.

equal to one eye, and the height to two eyes, measuring parallel to the eyebrows (fig. 2). The eye is

16

composed of the ball, the sight, the lacrymal point (which is the point nearest the nose), the upper and lower eyelids, and the eyebrow (fig. 3). The ball when seen in front, is an exact circle, with the sight in the centre; the height is equal to half the width, and the eyebrow is situated above the eyelid about one third the length of the eye. The eye in profile is half the length and exactly the same height as when seen in front; the eyeball forms an ellipse and the sight is always in the center (fig. 4). The ear in width is equal to one eye and its length to two eyes (fig. 5). In fig. 6 a front view of the face is given.

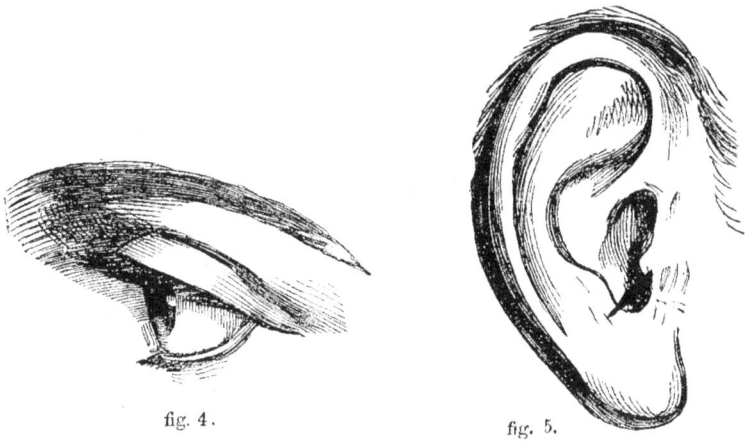

fig. 4 .   fig. 5.

In order to obtain a correct proportion, a perpendicular line must first be drawn, and the divided into two parts by a horizontal line drawn across the center of it, which will give the point for the height of the eyes. After drawing the outline of the face, the perpendicular line must be divided as in the sketch: the lower point will give the place for the lower part of the nose; the mouth is situated about half an eye lower than this; the ear is exactly the same length as the nose; consequently these are on a level. The same proportions are obtained in the figures 7, 8, 9, and 10. The hand is the same length as the face, and its width is equal to one-half (fig. 11). The side view of the hand is the same length as when seen in front (fig. 12). The foot in profile is nine eye in length and three in height (fig. 13). Figures 14 to 17 inclusive are examples of hands, arms, &c. &c.

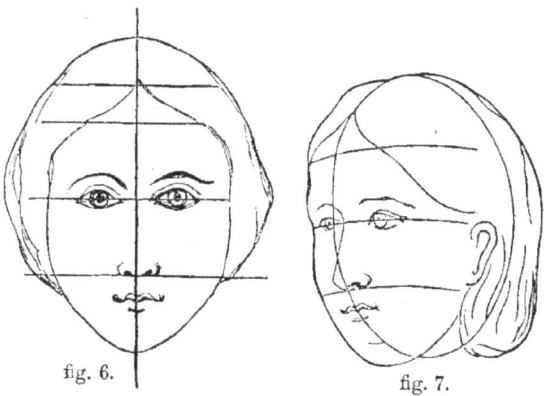

fig. 6.   fig. 7.

17

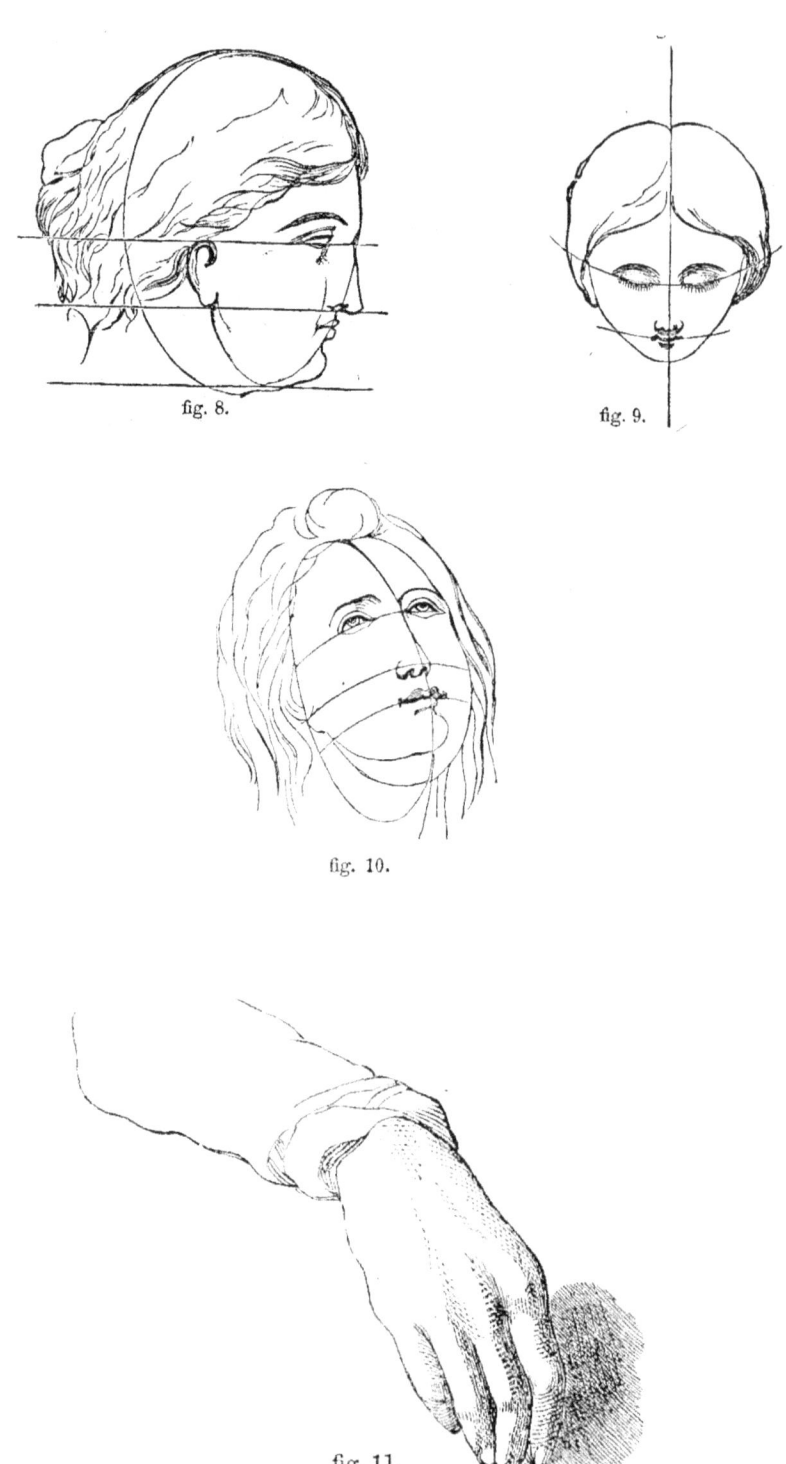

fig. 8.

fig. 9.

fig. 10.

fig. 11.

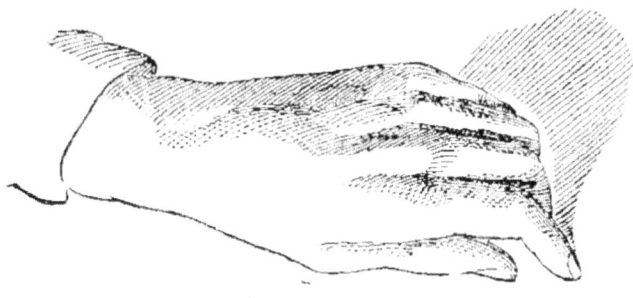

fig. 12.

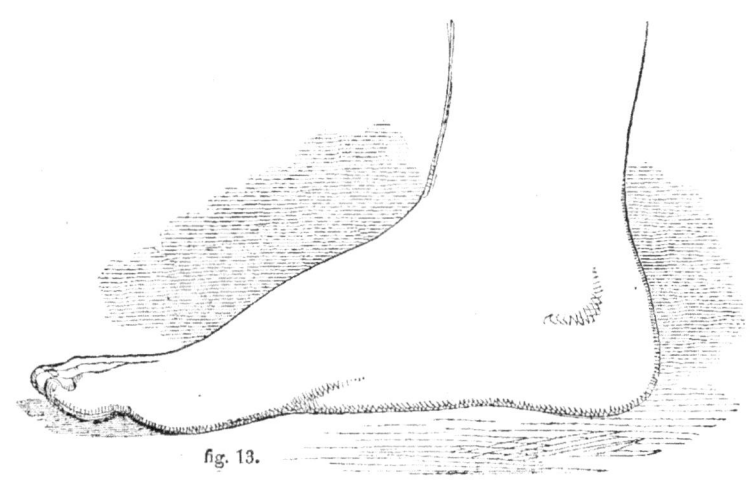

fig. 13.

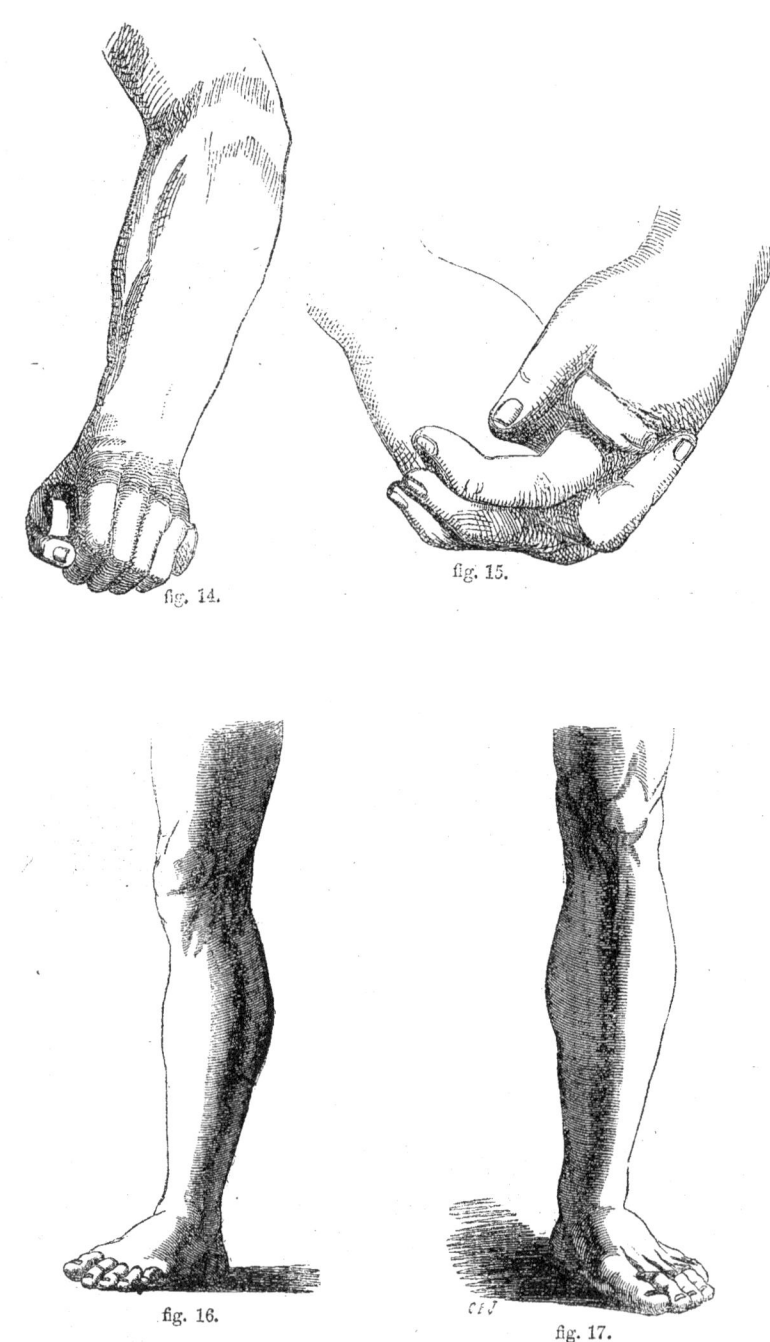

fig. 14.

fig. 15.

fig. 16.

fig. 17.

The generally received proportion of a man is ten faces in height; by extending the arms horizontally their full length, the same proportion is obtained. The length of two noses gives the width of the neck when seen in front. Two heads give the width of the shoulders when seen in front. The length of the forearm to the extremity of the fingers is equal to seven noses and a half. The width of the wrist is equal to a nose and one-third. When seen in front, the width of the knee is equal to two noses; but in profile it is a degree less. The length of the leg from the knee to the heel is equal to three faces. When viewed in front, the width of the leg near the ankle I equal to a nose and a half, but it is less when viewed in profile. The annexed (fig.18) is a sketch of a leg foreshortened and the following (fig. 19) that of the bust. In figures 20 and 21 are given examples of figure-drawing, which the pupil would do well to copy.

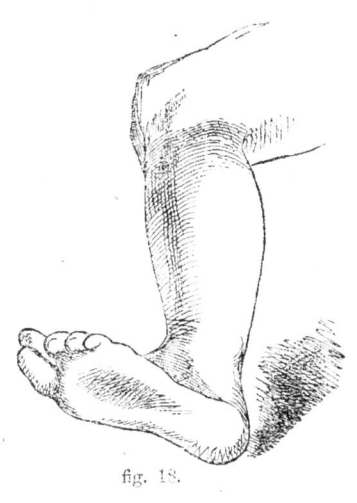

fig. 18.

At this stage of his progress the pupil should procure a plaster cast of the human figure or part of it. The materials he will require are, a drawing board on which to fix his paper, a few sticks of black chalk, a leather stump, a small quantity of charcoal, and a port crayon; it would also be well if he obtained a quantity of the crayon paper, which is slightly tinted, and takes the chalk well.

The light should be allowed to fall on the sketch from the left hand (It is from the right in fig. 19) In order to catch the proper effect of the parts sketched, the pupil should sit so as to throw back the head as far as possible from the drawing. A correct outline of the bust or figure should first be drawn with the charcoal, which may be erased by slightly brushing it with a silk or other light handkerchief; this is better than rubbing the lines out, as friction destroys the surface of the paper. After a correct outline of the subject is obtained, the pupil should trace it with the black chalk as faintly as possible, the by means of the handkerchief, remove the charcoal, which will leave a beautifully clear outline; after this he may begin the shading. He must first scrape a little of the chalk on the paper as fine as possible, and

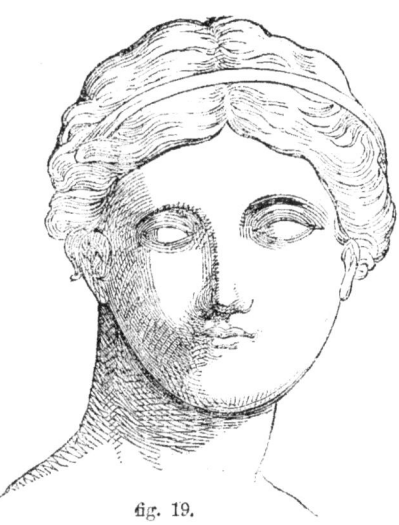

fig. 19.

run the leather stump among it; taking this, he must rub in the shadows; these will by this means be soft and beautiful, an will prepare a good ground for the finish. Having rubbed in the shading as like that of the model as possible, carefully observing the different strength of the shadows, he must point or sharpen his chalk, and begin to put in the details. He should patch over all the shading with the fine point of his chalk; this, when done in a proper manner, gives a very beautiful effect In shading the pupil must observe that there are two kinds of shadows; one is called the *shadow of incidence*, the other the *shadow of projection*: the shadow of projection is always defined, having a sharp decided edge; the shadow

21

of incidence is always soft, having no defined edge, but softening imperceptibly into the lights. The pupil must be careful to leave no hard edges; for although the shadow of projection is decided, the edges are not hard; moreover, the deepest shadows are always nearest the highest lights. The drawing of the bust or figure will require a slight background to detach it from the paper. If any mistakes are made in sketching, a little stale bread will remove the defective parts.

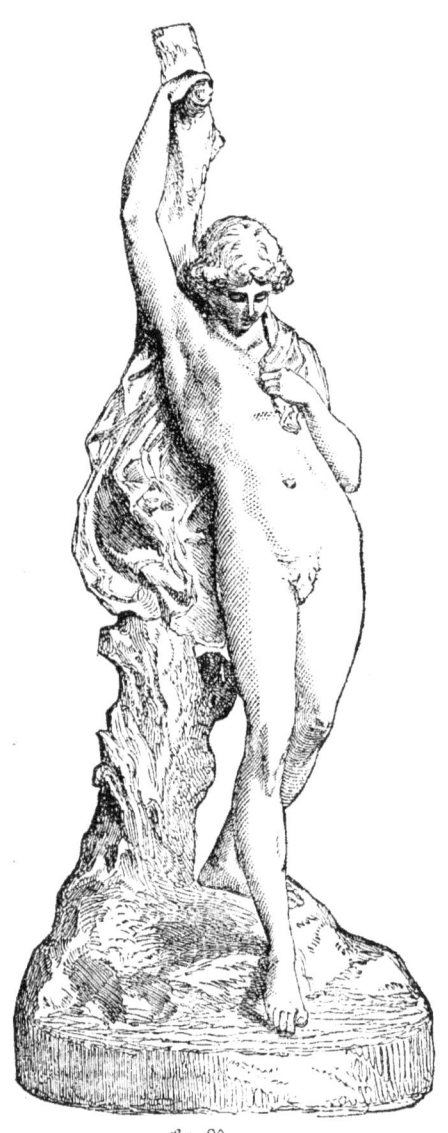

fig. 20.

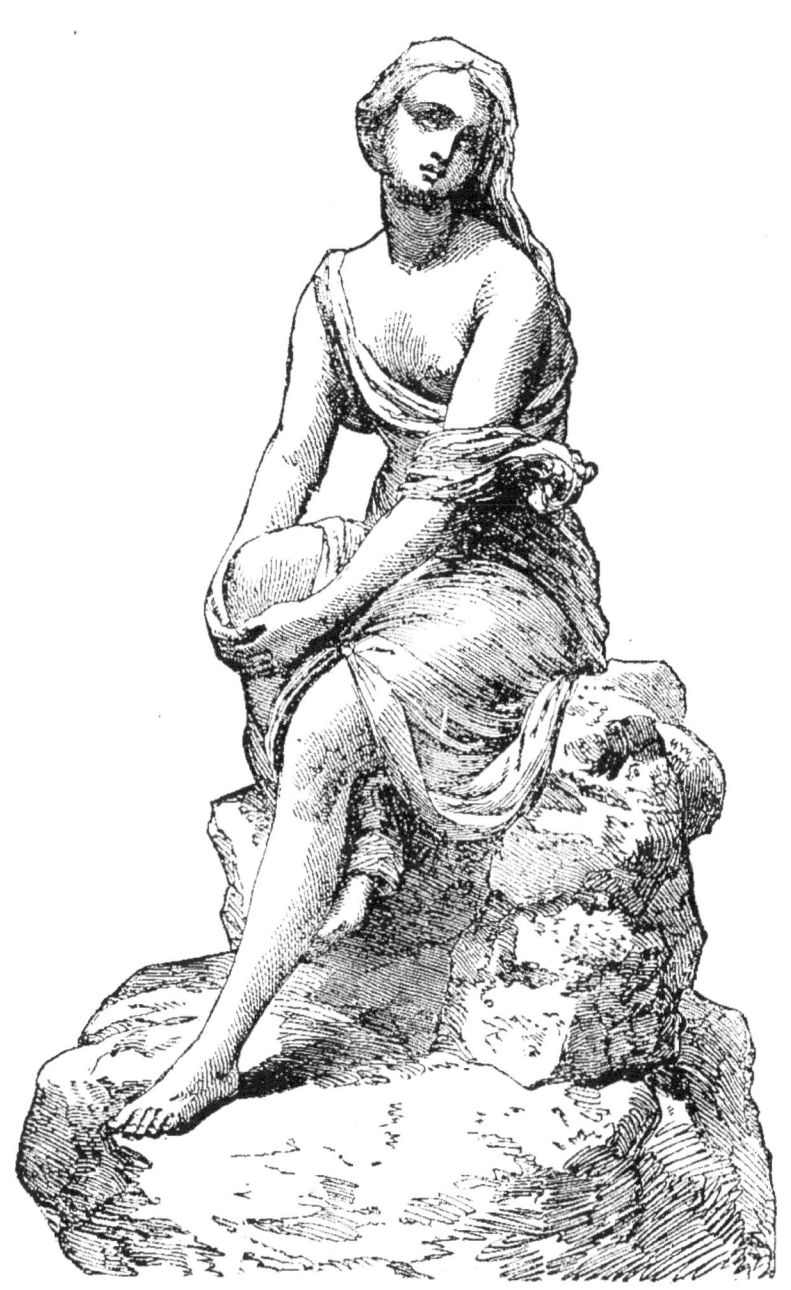

fig. 21.

THE YOUNG ARTISTS ASSISTANT
IN THE ART OF DRAWING
By Thomas Smith

This book was written by Thomas Smith. The full title is: *The Young Artist's Assistant in the Art of Drawing in Water Colours exemplified in a course of Twenty-Nine Progressive Lessons on animals, fruit, flowers, still life, portrait, miniature, landscape, perspective, architecture and sculpture calculated to afford those who are unacquainted with the art, the means of acquiring a competent knowledge without the aid of a master; being the only work of the kind in which the principles of effect are explained in a clear, methodical, and at the same time, familiar style.*

The book includes many colored woodblock plates demonstrating painting techniques, but what is reproduced here are the sections on figure drawing.

Before the ground work of any art or science can be considered as safely laid, the student must be made acquainted with its first principles and elements; and in none is this more requisite than in the elegant art of drawing. This useful and pleasing acquirement is base on the principles of geometry; the student must therefore, practice himself in drawing straight and curve lines, with ease and freedom, upwards and downwards, sideways, to the right or left and in any direction whatever. He should then learn to draw accurately, by command of hand only, squares, circles, ovals and other geometrical figures, The utility of following this preparatory course is demonstrated form the art of writing. The learner who, in his early progress in that art, has been well versed in text-hand writing, and in a free bold use of his pen, generally produces the finest specimens of calligraphy in the current affairs of life. So the student who, in his initiation in the art of drawing, has been practiced in the delineation of geometrical figures, by command of hand, acquires a free, bold, manner of designing. Nor is this all; he is enables to form just conceptions of proportion, distance and the like; and, consequently, is qualified to imitate, with greater ease and accuracy, the appearances of nature and of art.

This remark leads to one of equal importance on the subject of "Figure Drawing." In this most difficult part of the art you must proceed gradually and by parts. Never attempt to draw a whole figure at once. The sure method to attain proficiency in this or any other branch of the art, is to begin to practice its elements, and to make yourself perfectly master of one member before you proceed to another. Thus as the human body consists of various members of the eyes, ears, legs, arms, hands, feet, nose, mouth &c. you should first copy good specimens of those members, carefully imitating their various postures and actions, so as not only to avoid all sameness and imperfection, but also to give the life and spirit. In these sketches, (see the specimens annexed), always draw by command of hand only: never make use of lines and measures; but measure distances and proportions with your finger or pencil, and the judge them by the eye, which by degrees may be brought to judge of truth and proportion, with as much accuracy as if you applied your compasses, and recollect not to finish perfectly (a rule universally to be observed in all subjects), at first, any single part, but to sketch out faintly, and with slight strokes of the pencil, the shape and proportion of the whole member, with the action and turn of it; and after considering carefully, whether this first sketch be perfect, and altering it where it is amiss, you may proceed to finish the outline. Thus if you are sketching a hand or a foot, after having ascertained that your outline is correct, you may proceed to the bending of the joints, the knuckles, the veins, and other minutiæ By so doing you will not only sketch the shape and proportion of the member more easily, but also more perfectly. Another rule of primary importance is, accustom yourself to draw your figures sufficiently large, and not attempt to shadow any figure or object of any kind, until you have attained a tolerable proficiency in the use of your pencil.

The following are specimens for imitation of the various members of the human body.

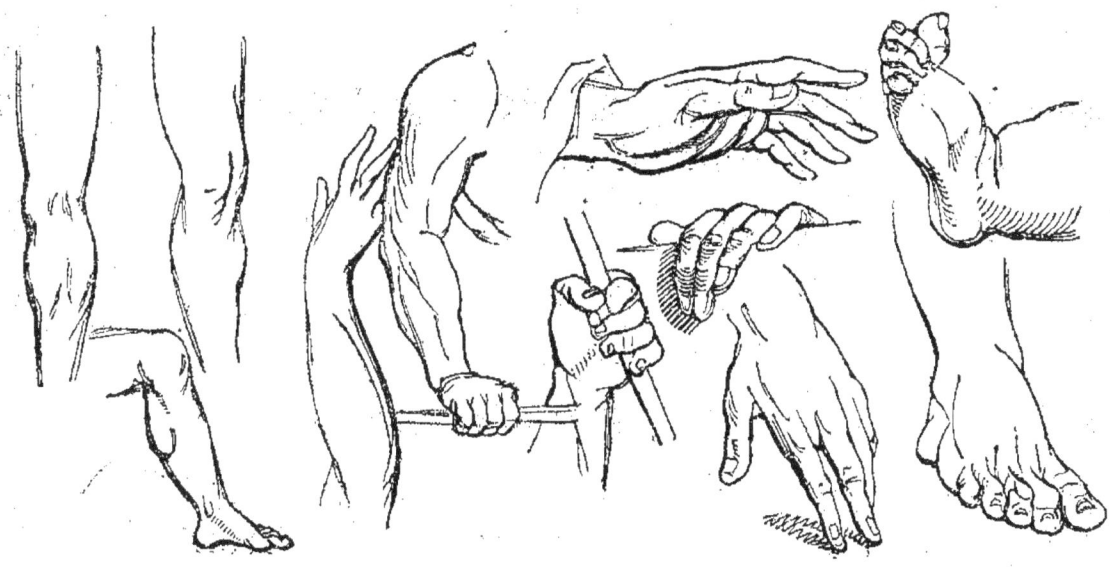

When you find yourself perfectly master of one member, proceed to another; and when you have gained a tolerable mastership of each, you may proceed to copy the "human face divine." In forming a perfect face your first business is to draw an oval or rather the form of an egg; in the middle of which, from top to bottom, draw a perpendicular line. Through the centre or middle of this line draw a diameter line, directly across from one side to the other of your oval as in examples *a a*. On these two lines all the features of the face are to be place as follows: the first must be allotted to the hair of the head; the second is from the top of the forehead to the top of the nose between the eyebrows; the third is from thence to the bottom of the nose; and the fourth includes the lips and the chin. Your diameter line, or the breadth of the face, is always supposed to be the length of five eyes; you must therefore divide it into five equal parts, and place the eyes upon it so as to leave exactly the length of one eye betwixt them. This is to be understood only of a full front face, for if it turn to either side, then distances are to be lessened on that side which turns from you, less or more, in proportion to its turning, as in the examples *b b b*. The top of the ear is to rise parallel to the eyebrows, at the end of the diameter line; and the bottom of it must be equal to the bottom of the nose. The nostrils ought not to come out farther than the corner of the eye in any face; and the middle of the mouth must always be placed upon the perpendicular line.

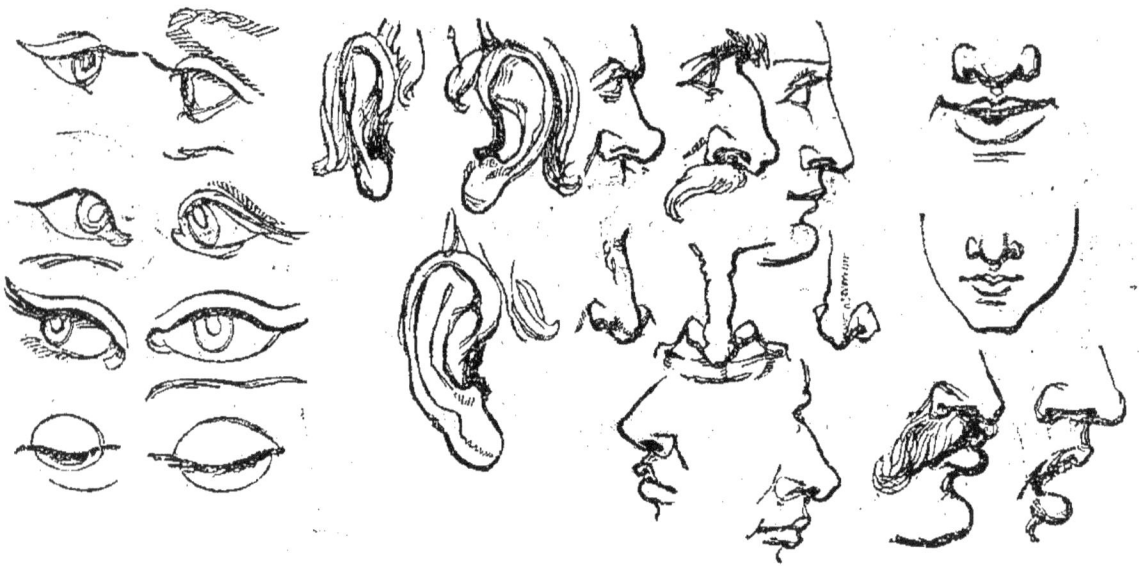

The following are specimens of this portion of the human frame.

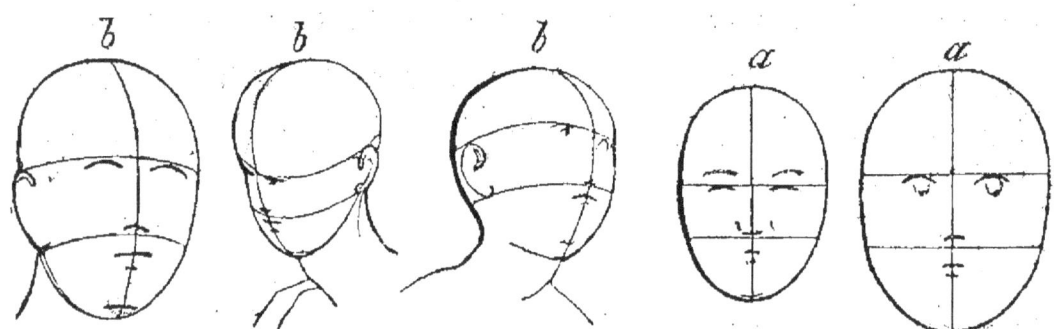

When the pupil is become tolerably expert in drawing faces, heads, hands and feet, he may next attempt to draw the whole of the human figure at length. In order to do this, let him first sketch the head; then draw a perpendicular line from the bottom of the head seven times its length (for the length of the head is about one-eighth part of the length of the figure). The best proportioned figures of the ancients are 7¾ heads in height. If, therefore, the figure stands upright, draw a perpendicular line from the top of the head to the heel, which must be divided into two equal parts. The bottom of the belly is exactly the centre. Divide the lower part into two equal parts again, the middle of which is the middle of the knee. For the upper part of the figure, the method must be varied. Take off with your compasses the length of the face (which is three parts in four of the length of the head); from the throat pit to the pit of the stomach is one face, from thence to the navel is another, and from thence to the lower rim of the belly is a third. The line must be divided into seven equal parts. Against the end of the first division place the breasts; the second comes down to the navel; the third to the extremity of the trunk; the fourth to the middle of the thigh; the sixth to the lower part of the calf; the seventh to the bottom of the heel, the heel of the bearing leg being always exactly under the pit of the throat. But as the essence

26

of all drawing consists in making at first a good sketch, the learner must in this particular be very careful and accurate; he ought to draw no one part perfect or exact till he sees whether the whole draught if good; and when he has altered that to his mind, he may then finish one part after another as exactly as he is able.

With regard to the proper order and manner of proceeding in drawing the human body. You must sketch the head first; then the shoulders in the exact breadth; then take the trunk of the body, beginning with the arm pits, (leaving the arms till afterwards,) and so draw down to the hips on both sides; and be sure to observe the exact breadth of the waist. When you have done this, draw that leg on which the body stands, and then the other which stands loose; then the arms, and last of all the hands. You must take notice also of the bowings and bendings that are in the body, making the part which is opposite to that which bends correspond to it; if the back bend in, the belly must stick out; if the knee bend out, the ham must fall in; and so of any other joint in the body. Finally, you must endeavor to form all the parts of the figure with truth, and in just proportion: not one arm or one leg bigger or less than the other: not broad Herculean shoulders, with a thin and slender waist; nor raw and bony arms, with thick and gouty legs: but let there be a kind of harmonious agreement amongst the members, and a beautiful symmetry throughout the whole figure.

The following sketches will assist in forming a just conception of the various attitudes and proportions of the human frame, in the periods of childhood and manhood.

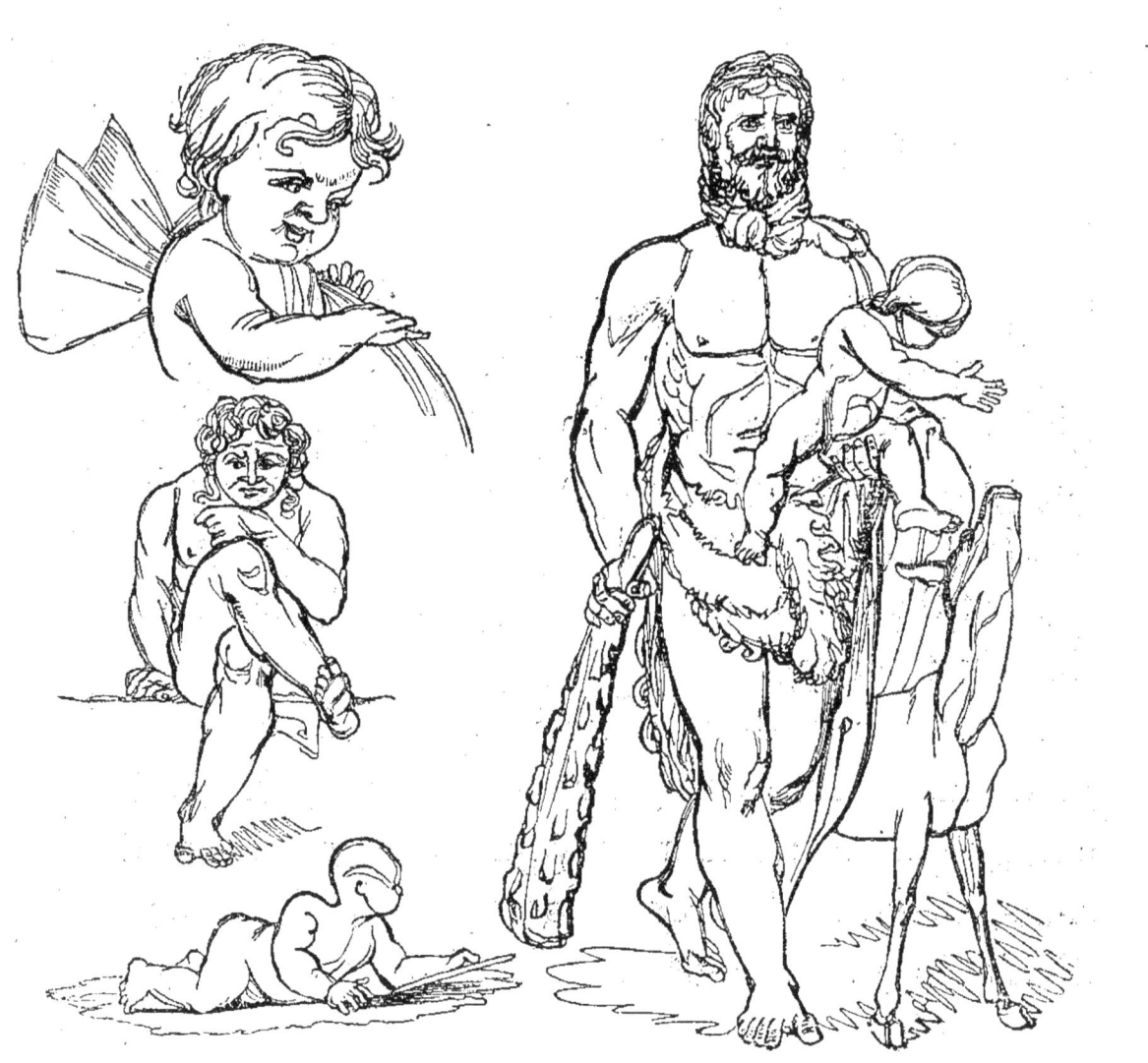

On Historical or Figure Drawing.

I now enter upon the highest and most difficult department of the art, that of drawing the human figure, in studying which the student ought to possess a number of plaster casts after the antique, such as

> The Apollo Belvedere
> The Venus de Medicis
> The Hercules
> The Antinous
> The Gladiator
> The Laocoon, &c. &c.

Should it not be in his power to procure these, the best prints after the old masters will be found serviceable, though it will be much better if he can commence his studies by drawing from the antique. The figure I should recommend is the Gladiator, though I would advise the student to begin by drawing the extremities, such as the hands and feet; after which he may proceed to draw faces till he have acquired a certain capability of representing these parts, when he may proceed with the whole length of the figure, in doing which he will find the following list of proportions of the human figure, taken principally from Hamilton's Drawing-Book, extremely useful.

The length of the head, neck, and trunk, is half of the entire height of the figure.
The lower extremities form the other half.
The entire height of the figure is ten times the length of its face, which begins at the lowest hairs of the forehead, and ends at the chin.
From the top of the head to the forehead is one-third of a face.
The face is divided into three equal parts, of which one contains the forehead, the next the nose, and the third the mouth and chin.
From the chin to the pit between the two collar bones at the bottom of the neck, two-thirds of a face.
From the bottom of the neck to the bottom of the breast, one face.
The remaining part of the trunk two faces.
The thigh down to the middle of the knee, two faces and a quarter.
From the middle of the knee to the ankle, two faces and a quarter.
From the ankle to the sole of the foot, half a face.
A man, when his arms are stretched out, is, from the longest finger of his right hand to the longest finger of his left hand, as broad as he is high.
From one side of his breast to the other, two faces.
From the shoulder to the elbow, two faces.
From the elbow to the root of the little finger, two faces.
From the point of the shoulder to the pit between the two collar bones, one face.
The foot is one-sixth the length of the figure.
The length of the face and hands ought to be equal.
In drawing children, the whole length ought to be equal to five heads, whereof the head and trunk take three, whilst the thighs and legs take the other two.
In drawing an man and a woman, the principal differences will be in the relative breadth of the shoulders and hips, which in the woman will be very nearly the same breadth, the

hips being very little narrower than the shoulder, whilst in the man the latter are considerably broader than the former.

In drawing a full face, the diameter across the eyes is equal to five lengths of an eye.

The distance between the eyes is equal to one eye.

The breadth of the nostrils, one eye.

The length of the mouth, two eyes.

The above rules the student will find extremely serviceable in correcting the first rough outline of a figure; by these rules he can also determine where the knee, foot, &c. of any figure ought to be placed after he has sketched the head.

In drawing plaster casts it is the custom to use grey paper, on which the figure is finished, with black and white chalk, making use of soft willow charcoal to sketch the first outline*. Chalk drawings are finished in two different ways; in the first the chalk is laid on in a succession of short strokes or hatches, seldom, if ever, using the stump to soften the edges of the shadows. This method has a very beautiful effect is well done, which, however, is far from compensating for the immense waste of time which finishing in this manner occasions. In the second the stump is in continual use to lay in, flatten, and soften the different shades; and thought the drawing is by no means so agreeable to the sight as those done in the former method, yet the facility and quickness with which the sketch of any figure is finished, amply makes up for its deficiency n other respects; for I always suppose that the pupil studies the figure for the sake of learning to draw it correctly, and not to acquire a capability of laying a number of lines together in a beautiful manner.

The annexed plate represents the portrait of a lady drawing in chalk, and finishing with the stump, in copying which the student must begin by drawing a faint outline with willow charcoal. When he has got this perfectly correct, he must efface it as much as he possibly can by passing a silk handkerchief lightly over it, or by rubbing it very gently with bread till it be scarcely visible; this being done, he must retrace the lines with hard black chalk**, and then begin by laying in the shadows of the chalk of a middling degree, working them soft and flat by running them with the stump; this must be repeated till all the dark shades are of a proper depth, and nothing remains to be done but the very black touches,which must be laid in with vigour, using the blackest chalk; and the bright lights, which must be put on with the white chalk softened with the stump, in using which take care that it be not with the end which has softened the black shades, a you would otherwise make a shade instead of a light.

---

*   Charcoal is used in preference to chalk on account of the facility with which it is effaced if incorrect: the student must recollect to use the crum of bred, which is at least one day old, instead of Indian rubber, to take out any parts which are not right.

** The student ought to provide himself with black chalk of three degrees of hardness, one being very soft and black, one in a middling degree, and one hard; one kind of white chalk will be sufficient.

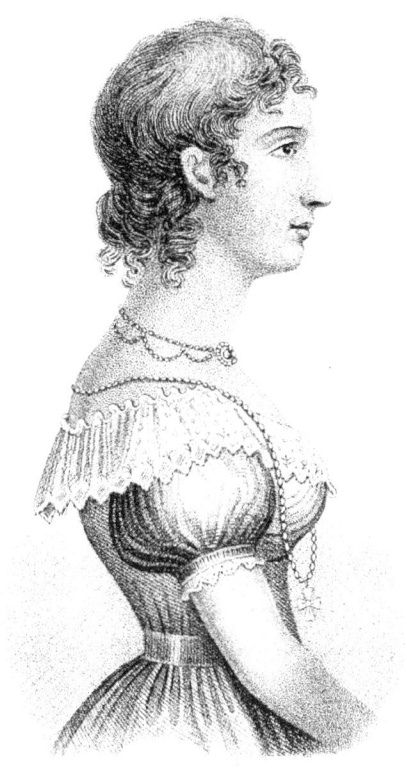

FIGURE DRAWING.

Pub.d by Sherwood, Jones & C.o June 1.1824.

In drawing the whole-length figure the student must first begin with the head, then proceed with the trunk, and lastly the lower extremities and arms—all these ought to be sketched lightly, and corrected till the proportions be tolerably correct, when he must observe whether the figure stand well on its feet, and whether the general attitude be easy and natural: this being done, he may again proceed to correct the proportion for the last time, after which he must draw in the strong outline, and then proceed to finish.

Beginners frequently find considerable difficulty in drawing from plaster casts, owing to their not knowing how to place them in the easiest position, as well as from injudicious manner in which they allow the light to fall upon them; I have also frequently found that young persons have a dislike to draw

31

from the antique, on account of the little interest that the subjects afford to those who are not sufficiently advanced in the art, to feel the beauty of the proportions which those figures exhibit. I n one of my pupils (a boy about ten years old), whose parents were desirous that he should study the figure, this dislike was invincible; I therefore made a number of copies from the Apollo, the Gladiator, Hercules, &c., on a rather small scale, the figures being about six inches high, and placed them in different attitudes. I also gave then appropriate dresses, representing them as fitting tight to the body and limbs, so that the form might be seen as well as if they were without them: to each also I gave a character best sited to their attitudes, making an archer of the Apollo, a soldier of the Gladiator, &c. &c. With these my pupil was wonderfully delighted, and copied them several times over, for the archer's green jacket and the red coat of the soldier excited an interest which could never have been caused by the beautiful proportions of the Apollo Belvedere and the Gladiator. By thus giving him drawings from plaster, each disguised in modern dresses, I led him through the whole range of antique figure, and made him well acquainted with their proportions long before he had the least idea of the deception (if it merit the name) which had been practiced upon him.

The study of all the anatomy which is required in drawing, and which consists of nothing more than a capability of drawing the skeleton and the external muscles, together with a knowledge of the uses of the latter, is so trifling, that I should advise every person to acquire it who wishes to draw the figure correctly. A variety of works have been published for this purpose, some of which may be obtained at a very moderate expense.

For those who wish to study the figure merely for the purposes of introducing it in landscape, the best work is Pyne's Rustic Figures, published by Ackerman in the Strand: in this the student will find all that he an possibly require in landscape painting.

A GUIDE TO FIGURE DRAWING
By G. E Hicks

G. E. Hicks wrote *A Guide to Figure Drawing*, it was published by George Rowney & Co. who sold artist's materials which were advertised extensively in the back of the book. That did not prevent it from being a useful tool and an interesting explanation of the arts of the time. Reproduced here are chapters on the antique, the living figure, and part of the chapter on expression.

THE ANTIQUE

In this chapter on the principles of Outline the Pupil was directed how to draw a line with correctness and decision. He must now learn to apply his proficiency to the drawing of the figure; and, to commence with, portions of it may be copied from drawings in outline in the following way, a method which need not be discontinued in any future state of proficiency.

Before drawing in the detail it is necessary to find out the general form of the object and the space it is to occupy on the paper.

This may be done by regarding the angular mass without meaning, and as such to represent it, straight line being carried from one prominent point to another, giving it the appearance of a block of marble before the chisel has indicated the intended form. Examples of thus drawing "in the square" are given in Plates 5 and 6, from the face and foot.

In Plate 6 the method is exemplified in its different stages; fig. 1 showing the general form and intended size of the drawing, in the marking out of which great care must be taken, as subsequent accuracy depends very much upon it; fig. 2 shows the same further carried out, the more minute parts being formed in the same way; in fig. 3 the rounded form has been drawn.

The actual measurement of the individual parts will be of little assistance, as the slightest movement of position will alter it. Their relative size, therefore, as they appear to the eye, is our only guard in this case.

This may be ascertained by holding the pencil of crayon at arms length, and measuring the proportions on it with the thumb, and, turning it, by comparing on part with another.

To begin, then. Having first pinned or stretched a piece of paper in a board, ascertain the width of the object in comparison to its height; then mark the same relative measurements on the paper according to the intended size of the drawing. Next sketch in the general shape of the mass, as in Plate 6, fig. 1, and, as the detail may have a tendency to confuse, its effect may be counteracted by half closing the eyes. Before proceeding any further, it would be well to go over this again and again, and correcting anything the may be wrong, as the feeling and action of any figure depend upon this stage of the drawing. It may be then carried to the same state as Plate 6, fig 2; and in marking out the detail in the square, if the most prominent part be first drawn correctly there will be no difficult in adding the remainder.

PLATE 5.

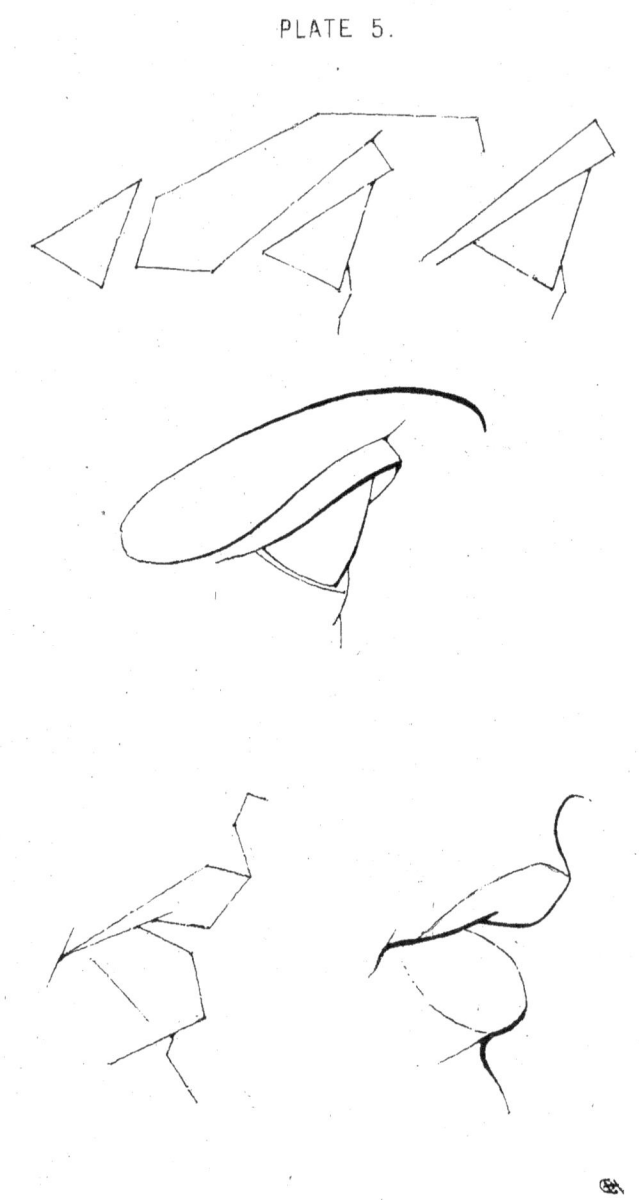

PLATE 6.

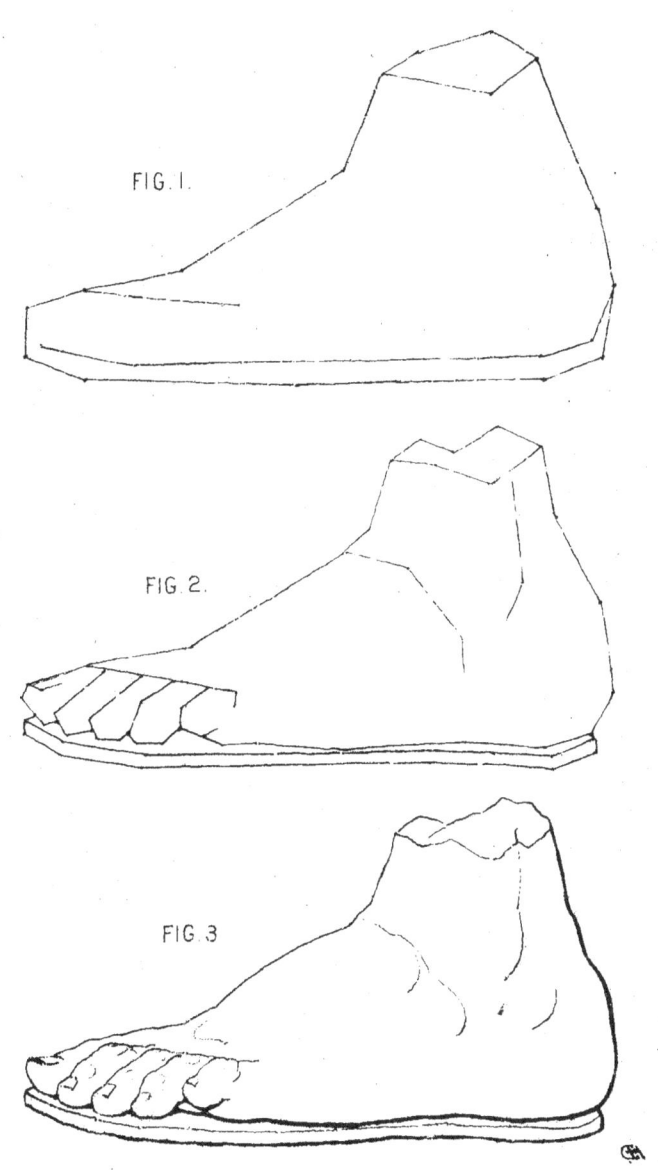

FIG. 1.

FIG. 2.

FIG. 3

If this plan is followed out, the student will find that he has been spared much uncertainty and confusion, and that he will have little difficulty in completing the drawing by introducing the rounded, in the place of straight lines. The pencil can be held before the model in the same position as the lines drawn, by which deviation of the round may be more easily observed.

If a finished outline is desired, the lines representing the undersides may be strengthened, as I Plate 6, fig 3; but if a shaded drawing, the whole must be left in a delicate state.

In drawing the whole figure more difficulty will be experienced in representing the feeling and proportions correctly. It will be useless to sketch the character and expression first, as they will be destroyed subsequently in the correction of innumerable mistakes. The drawing must be commenced in a business-like manner, and marked out with mathematical precision; and so correctness in this first stage will be encouraging throughout, and on this foundation may be safely added all the finish and expression that can be desired; for without correctness of outline expression is either and affectation or a caricature.

Let us take, for illustration, such a figure as that in Plate 8. The model must be placed at the distance of two or three time its height from the eye, and so situated in regard to the light that its shadow may be its own length. It is to be drawn two feet in height, and upon measurement its length is found to be eight heads. Mark off either an eighth of the whole or three inches from the top, for the length of the head. Put marks, also, to divide the figure into eight equal parts. Ascertain, then, the width of the head compared with its height, or with any portion of the figure, and draw it in the square correctly. With this starting point it will be comparatively easy to fix the position of the rest. Take a plumb-line, or a thread with a weight on the end, and, holding it up at arm's length before the figure, see what prominent point falls under any portion of the head, and mark it accordingly, then ascertain by measurement how low it comes; and in this way several points may be fixed, which will be a sufficient guide for every part of the figure.

Should the position of the figure be such as to prevent this plan being followed, the same assistance may be obtained by drawing first any principal division; or by ascertaining the central spot, and measuring the masses in relation to it.

This plan may appear to some too methodical or mechanical, and devoid of artistic feeling; but it is only necessary to point to the disproportion and struggling incorrectness of an outline drawn entirely "by the eye," to prove that such a feeling may be affected by the beginner, not only without benefit, but to the formation of an incurable habit. If artistic feeling exists at all in the mind, method only will pave the way for its proper exercise.

It is useless to begin shading before the outline is completed. Shade ought not to be made the refuge of ignorance and the screen of unnumbered errors, but the support of character and the perfective of expression.

The answer is, that shadow may assist in correcting the outline. But this is altogether false. The shaded part, instead of assisting the eye in judging of an outline, entirely perverts it. For instance, suppose a figure to be sketched in roughly, and the head shaded, the eye is upset at once, as the shaded part appears fuller and larger, and there is no longer like to compare with like, but outline with shade. The consequence will be that the parts subsequently drawn will be out of proportion.

There are few, however, who act upon this self-evident rule, the common practice being, perhaps from impatience, that of commencing to shade before the outline is finished.

PLATE 7.

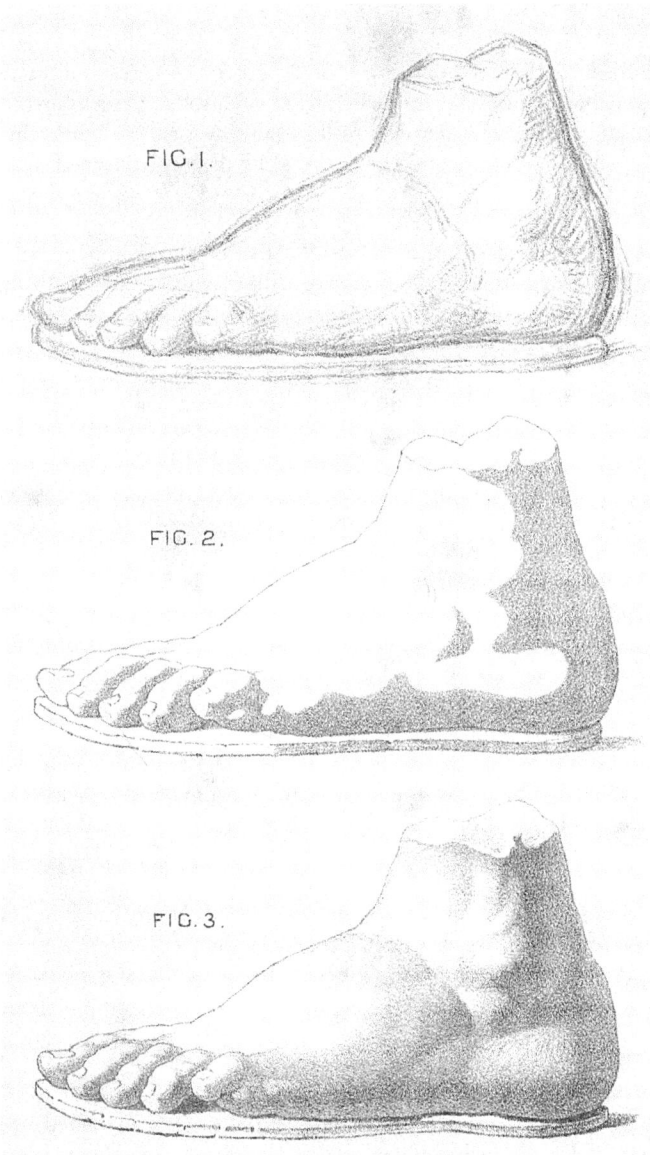

FIG. 1.

FIG. 2.

FIG. 3.

PUBLISHED BY G ROWNEY & C?. 52,RATHBONE PLACE.& 29.OXFORD ST. LONDON.

Again. It is said that if the whole figure be equally advanced, it will assist in correcting the outline; but let it be remembered that an object may be made to appear larger or smaller by the degree of half-tint on its receding parts; if, then, this is not perfectly correct, it will be of no assistance, and it

37

will be impossible to ascertain whether the outline or shadow is at fault. And, after all, why should the student travel by the most difficult road? Drawing is not so easy that he can afford to trifle himself in discovering the first principles by his failures in the second.

On the contrary, in outline, the drawing should be kept very dry and uninteresting until quite finished; and thus the eye, having nothing with which to satisfy itself, will feel sensitive to the least error; and, comparing one clean outline with another, will be able to arrive at the same conclusion. As a general rule, the outline should not be altered after the shading is commenced, for in all probability it will upset the whole figure.

The danger of the practice of thus modeling the figure without drawing it cannot be too strongly represented to the young student; the more so, as the English school, in its partiality for colour and light and shade, has neglected the more important study of outline, to the loss of expression of character, correctness of eye, and purity of taste, and has become the ridicule of its more rigid neighbours. outline, though only suggestive, is complete in its impression, and is able of itself to convey all of the higher qualities of art, form, action and expression; while color, light and shade, and composition are subservient to, and dependent on it.

If, then, Outline or the drawing of form has always been acknowledged by the highest authorities to be what Annibal Caracci termed it, "the beginning, the middle, and the end of art," might it not be well made a separate study for the Pupil, and proficiency in it, as a separate branch, be made as much an object of acquisition as the production of a well-shaded but untimely drawing? As no principle demands more attention than this, and none carries with it a richer reward, the Student would find that in extending its application to the varied forms and actions of the human figure, and to the expression of the affections and passions, he has obtained a correctness of eye and steadiness of hand which he would have vainly sought in any other way.

We now come to the shading of the figure, and some attention is required in placing it so that part of it may be in shadow and part (two-thirds) in light; and the window, which should face the north, and consequently unaffected by the sun, situated at such a height as to produce a shadow as long as the figure is high.

In the chapter on Outline, reference was made to its becoming modified under the influence of partial light. Indeed, we are now no longer to consider the outline as such, but merely as the boundary of the shadow; and so great is this modification and blending of parts, that it is a common expression that no outline is to be seen in nature.

The plan which will most assist the beginner is that of laying in the broad shadows, as in Plate 7, fig. 2, with a dark flat equal tint, after having outlined them correctly. This will greatly assist in judging of the comparative depth of the half-tints, and can be readily darkened or lightened as occasion may require. This will act as a register; and some such guide is necessary to one unaccustomed to the work, for without it he will be surprised to find how weak every part of the drawing will look, and will feel discouraged in having to go over the whole of it again.

Discouragement should be cheated away by every possible means, for although the pursuit is in itself delightful, the road which leads to it is necessarily tedious; and as the hand cannot work well unless the mind is in good humour, whatever tends to irritate it should be avoided ; and this is the reason why so much stress is laid on the Pupil following a given plan; not that the advanced Student cannot obtain an equally good drawing without it, but that he may be carried through the first stages by the surest steps, and at the same time be made thoroughly acquainted with its principles.

If tinted paper is used, the high-lights may now be put in sparingly with white chalk, confining them as much as possible to spots. (Plate 7, fig. 2.) The lights are required in this stage of the drawing as an additional guide for the half-tints, on which depends in a great measure the beauty of the drawing, as the shading must not approach too near them, the color of the paper being allowed to represent the more delicate tints.

If the paper is white, a back-ground may be made of a flat half-tint. A figure on white paper requires a tint behind it, otherwise the lights lose their value, the shadows their delicacy, and therefore the figure its relief. This tint should be darker than the light masses and lighter than the shadows. To give additional relief the back-ground may be darkest behind the lightest part of the figure and *vice versa*, but this does not necessarily add to its grace or grandeur.

Now follows the toning or half-tint, and in doing this it must be remembered that no lines are apparent in natural shadow, and that therefore while the shading must be made to appear smooth at a little distance, the lines which compose it should be carried in the direction of the surface and thereby assist in indicating form.

Nor must any hard strokes be seen, but the lights and shadows must be lost in each other without any apparent separation.

The degree of tint on the several parts of the body will be regulated by their position in regard to the light, the slightest inclination downwards or from the light in any direction will increase it; so that by the half-tints the exact inclination of the limbs must be determined.

It may be observed that if the head is erect the face will be gradually darker towards the chin, a fact which is very often overlooked, but without which it is almost impossible to obtain sweetness of expression.

The drawing now possesses all its softness and delicacy without strength, and to obtain this it only remains to add the depths and modify the broad-shadows. Shade is not a positive quality, but the absence of light, and therefore scarcely two depths will be similar; that nearest the eye will of course be the strongest, but the whole of the broad-shade will be affected more or less by reflections from the objects which surround it. (Plate 7, fig. 3.) *

---

*"The surfaces of globular or convex bodies have as great a variety of lights and shadows as the bodies that surround them."—Leonardo da Vinci.

PLATE 8.

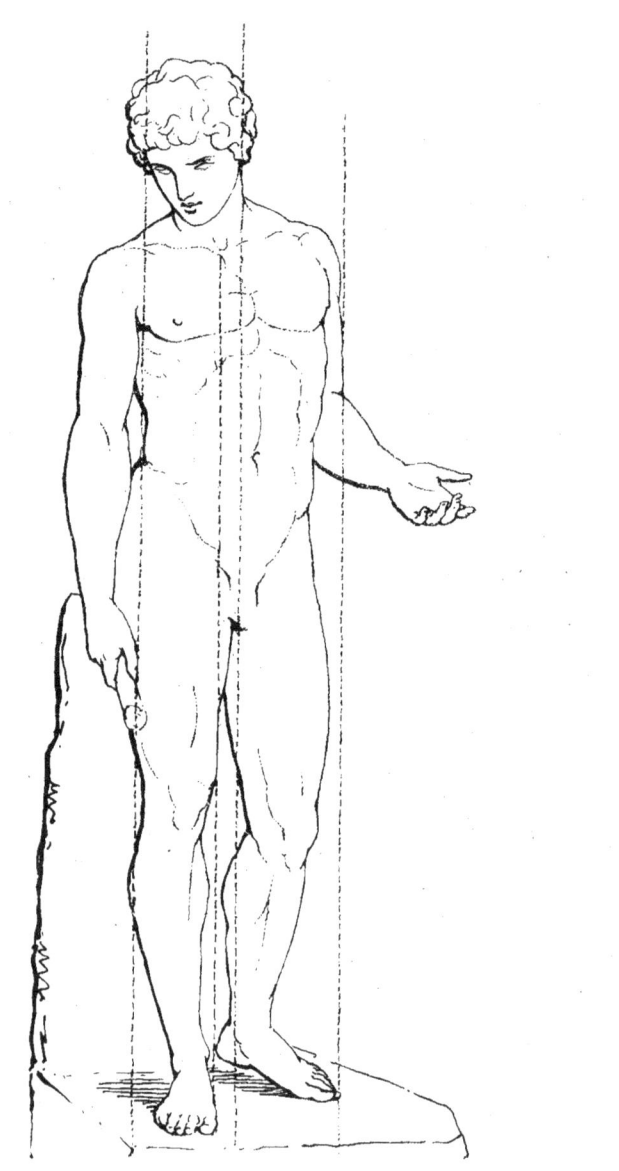

PRINTED & PUBLISHED BY G.ROWNEY & Cº 52,RATHBONE PLACE,& 29,OXFORD ST. LONDON.

PROPORTION

In making proportion the subject of a separate chapter, the Student is informed that his familiarity with it will have but little to do with his advancement in art. Volumes have been filled with accurate measurements which have no practical influence on the Student, and tend rather to confuse than to assist.** The general standard of proportion in the Antique may be given in small compass; deviations in the several statues being in accordance with their respective characters;— and as to nature, there are scarcely two individuals to be found who measure the same. It is like Perspective, simple enough in its general rules, but turned into a bugbear by its complicated criticisms and explanations. "From Vitruvius with his commentators and Leonardo da Vinci, to Albert Durer, Lomazzo, and Jerome Cardan,—from the corrected measurements of Du Fresnoy, and De Piles to Watelet, Winkleman and Lavater, it would be easy to show that the mass of variance, peculiarity, and contradiction greatly overbalances the coincidence of experiment and measure."†

It will be only necessary to give the general divisions, and although the painter should be familiar with these, he can only use them subject to the alterations caused by position and perspective.

The bodily ideal may be considered as an union of the essential and characteristic with the addition of the beautiful and sublime; or as it is expressed by Cicognara, "The ideal in art is nothing more than the imitation of an object as it ought to be in perfect nature, divested of the errors or distortions which secondary causes produce."

Now the realization of this is a gradual process developed only by the most accurate study and knowledge of nature. A combination of circumstances is also necessary in order to carry out this study with any success. The fittest subject for it is a race of men naturally well developed and trained from infancy in the constant but moderate use of natural exercises, with sufficient and regular food, and inhabiting a climate where the changes are not too sudden. And if we add to this the constant opportunity of witnessing the human frame under the influence of every exercise and feeling, and the familiarity with its action and appearance thus necessarily acquired; together with a highly educated perception of the beautiful, and a hand trained and able to transcribe it; we see at once the means by which Greece attained so high a standard of ideal form.

But in such a climate as that of England, and among a people of our habits, such opportunities are not attainable; and therefore, though thankful for the change, in this we must accede to the verdict which succeeding ages have passed, and submit to her as our instructor in the human form.

The average height of a full-sized male figure is about eight heads, the divisions falling consecutively on these points, viz., the chin, the fifth rib, the depression above the navel, the *os-pubis* or lower extremity of the trunk, the middle of the thigh, the knee, just above the ankle, and the sole of the foot.

**Five minutes, a foot rule, and a trained eye will do more to help than all the books in the world.

†   Fuselli.

The measurement of a few figures are here given, viz:—

	Heads.
The Apollo,	7⅞
Hercules, (Farnesian)	7⅞
Antinous,	7½
Laocoon,	7⁹⁄₁₆
Peace,	7 ½
Pyramus,	7½
Venus, (de Medici)	7¾
Shepherdess, (Grecian)	7⅞

The head may be divided into four parts, equal with the exception of the upper division, which is rather the shortest, viz., at the root of the hair, the root of the nose or the upper eye-lid, the bottom of the nose, and the chin.

The length of the eye is one fifth the width of the head.

The hand is as long as the face; and the foot one sixth or seventh of the body.

Narrow shoulders and wide hips are the distinguishing characteristics of the female figure; the male possessing wide shoulders and narrow hips.

The proportions of the living figure vary from seven to eight heads.

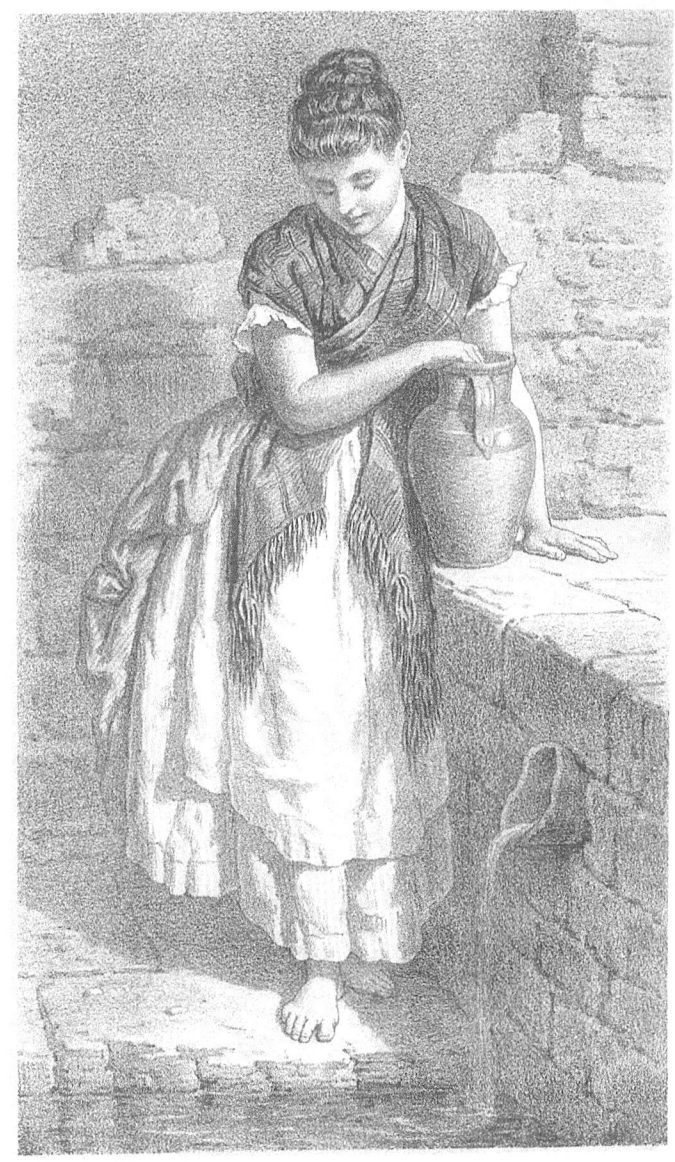

PUBLISHED BY G.ROWNEY & Cº 52,RATHBONE PLACE,& 29,OXFORD ST.LONDON.

PLATE 9.

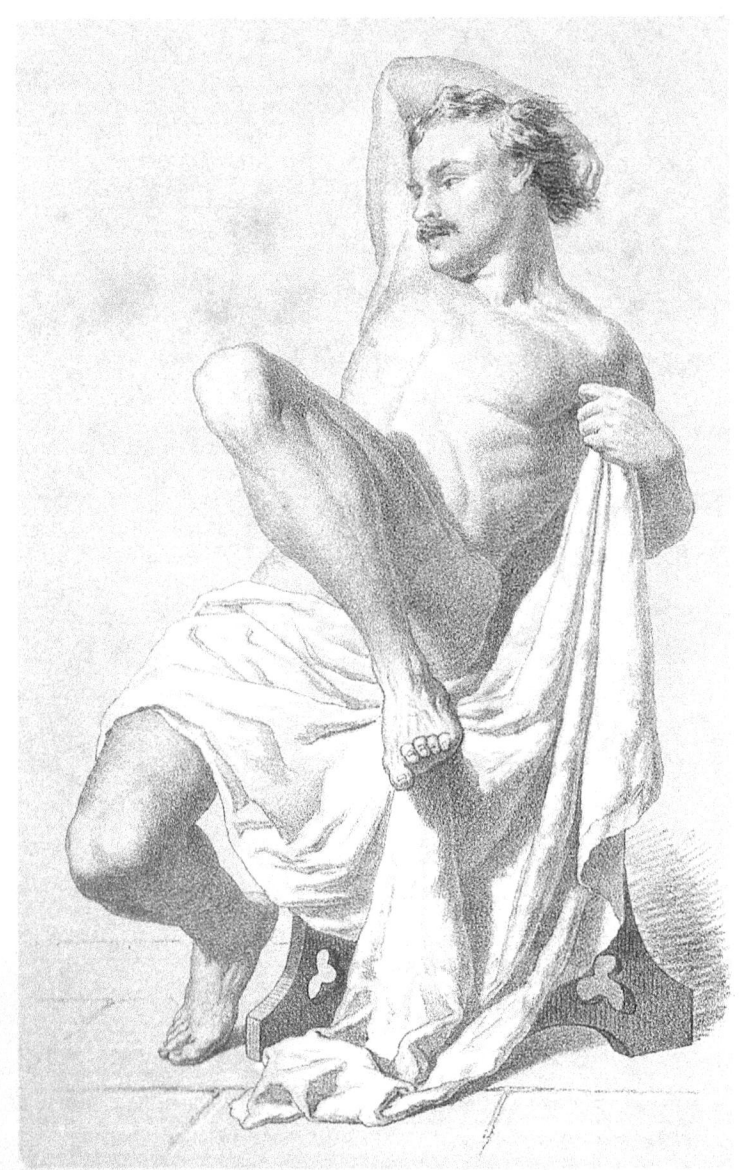

PUBLISHED BY G ROWNEY & C⁰ 52,RATHBONE PLACE,& 29,OXFORD ST LONDON.

The Oxford Drawing Book
or the
Art of Drawing
and the
Theory and Practice of Perspective
in a Series of Letters
By Nathaniel Whittock

The Oxford Drawing Book was published in 1840 and as the title says, takes the form of a series of letters to the student teaching the method of drawing, Lithographic illustrations were prepared especially for the book. Letters IX. and X. are addressed to drawing the human figure.

THE
OXFORD DRAWING BOOK,
OR THE
ART OF DRAWING,
AND THE
THEORY AND PRACTICE OF PERSPECTIVE,
IN A SERIES OF LETTERS
CONTAINING PROGRESSIVE INFORMATION ON
SKETCHING, DRAWING, AND COLOURING LANDSCAPE SCENERY, ANIMALS, AND THE HUMAN FIGURE;
WITH A
NEW METHOD OF PRACTICAL PERSPECTIVE:
DETAILED IN A NOVEL, EASY, AND PERSPICUOUS STYLE,
FOR THE USE OF TEACHERS, OR FOR SELF-INSTRUCTION.
BY NATHANIEL WHITTOCK,
TEACHER OF DRAWING AND PERSPECTIVE, AND LITHOGRAPHIST TO THE UNIVERSITY OF OXFORD.
EMBELLISHED WITH UPWARDS OF ONE HUNDRED LITHOGRAPHIC DRAWINGS,
FROM REAL VIEWS, TAKEN EXPRESSLY FOR THIS WORK.

A NEW AND IMPROVED EDITION.

NEW YORK:
PUBLISHED BY COLLINS, KEESE & CO.,
No. 254 PEARL STREET.
1840.

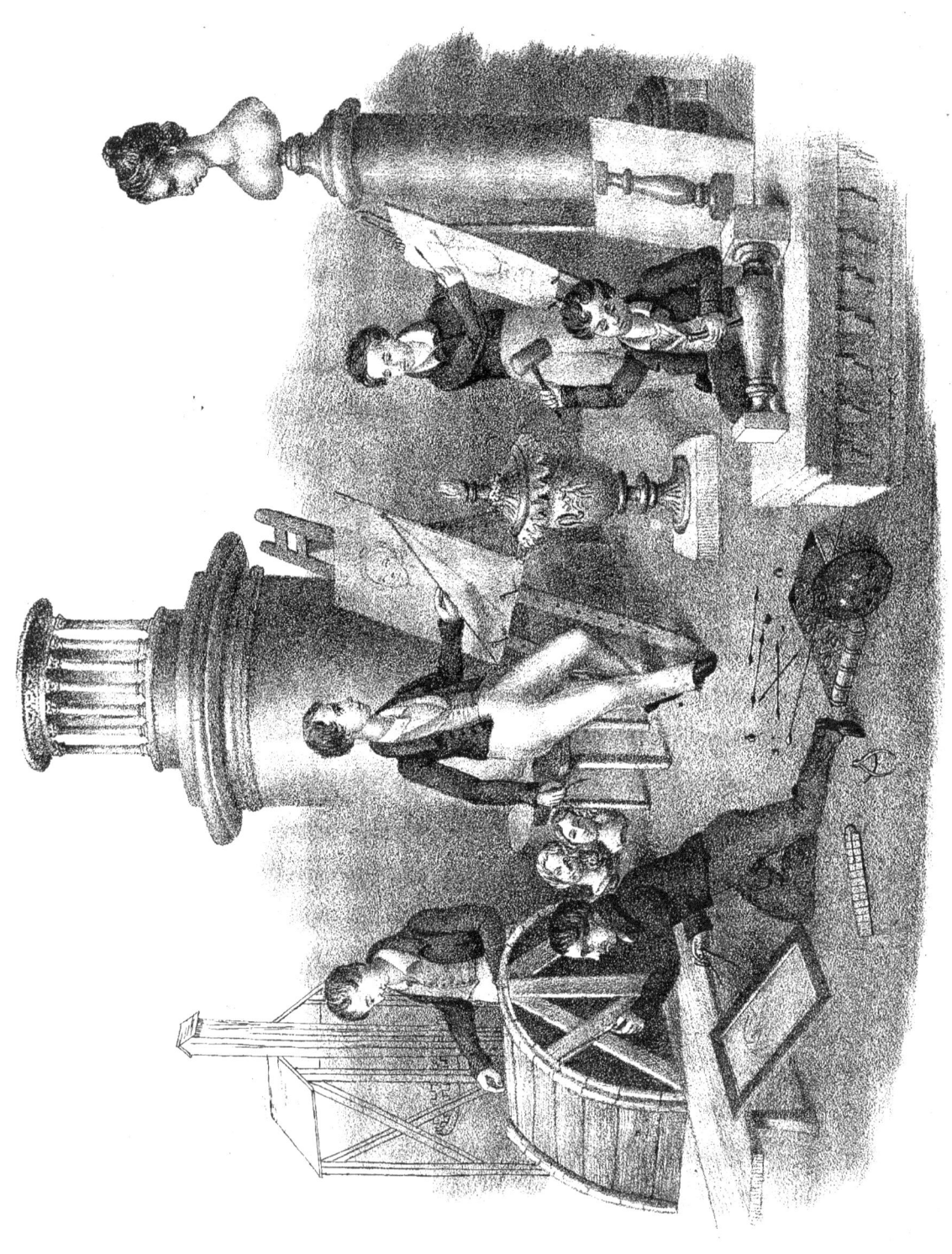

LETTER IX.

Nothing can surpass the beauty and symmetry of the human figure as we are told by our Creator that he dignified his last formed creature man by creating him "in his own image." Justly to delineate the "human form divine," is the highest point of excellence to which a painter can aspire. The study of this subject will therefore demand your undivided attention and persevering exertion.

Before we proceed to draw any particular limbs or feature, it is necessary the we should know properly where to place them. If I were addressing a person who contemplated making the art a profession, I should advise him to obtain a small work by Tinney*, displaying the anatomy of the human figure, written expressly for artists, and to make himself thoroughly acquainted with the names and forms of the bones and muscles , before he attempts to draw the figure. It is for want of this preliminary study, which is the only foundation for correctness, and which may be easily attained, that many persons fail who endeavour to obtain a livelihood by portrait painting. But as the study of anatomy would occupy much time for persons who make drawing an amusement only, certain rules have been laid down by eminent masters for the relative proportions of the human figure which will in some degree supply the place of anatomical knowledge.

We will commence our studies with the rules for producing the head and face. By referring to Plate LII. You will find that the first head is commenced by drawing an oval of rather the outline of the shape of an egg, it being larger at the top. Then draw a perpendicular line dividing the oval in the centre; this line in the plate I marked *a a*, and is crossed at equal distances by the lines *b b*, *c c*, and *d d*. The lines *c c*, and *d d*, are again divided into five parts. I have drawn this figure without the features being marked on it. See No. 1. Plate LIII. You will perceive that the crown of the head and part of the forehead occupy the first division as far as the line *b b*, thence to *c c*, is placed the part of the forehead seen below the hair, the eyebrows and eyelids; the eyes are always placed exact in the centre of the head, as may be seen on the line *c c*; the next division *d d*, gives the length of the nose; and the last is occupied by the mouth and chin. In the second and fourth of the perpendicular divisions, between the lines *c c*, and *d d*, the eyes are placed; and you will observe that the distance between the eyes is equal to the breadth of one eye; and that the same lines which mark the length of the nose, show the length of the ears. This diagram shows the general principles on which the head is designed in every possible position: and it will much lessen the difficulty, if you mark the different proportions with a pencil on an egg, adding features as in Plate LII. Y turning the egg in various directions, you can have a half or three-quarter face, and make it look upwards or downwards at pleasure: this will exemplify at once the reason why the lines in our succeeding examples curve in different directions according to the inclination of the head. As I before observed, these divisions of the head are only to supply the place of anatomical knowledge, and it is not to be supposed that all heads are formed with mathematical nicety, according to the foregoing rules. These general principles should always be kept in mind when drawing either from a copy or from life, and they will prevent your making and very glaring error. The drawing on your egg will enable you to form a second head in Plate LII.

---

*Compendium anatomicum, or, A compendious treatise of anatomy adapted to the arts of painting and sculpture: in which the external muscles of the human body are represented as they appear when cleared of the skin, the membrana adiposa, and the veins and arteries that lie on their surface : with a concise explanation shewing their names, their origin, their insertion, and their use : a work of very great service to painters, statuaries, and all professors of drawing and design : as well as a proper introduction to the study of anatomy for the use of young surgeons : and so contrived as to be both an ornamental and instructive furniture for surgeon's studies, &c., John Tinny, Printed for John Tinney engraver and printseller, 1743

Pl.52

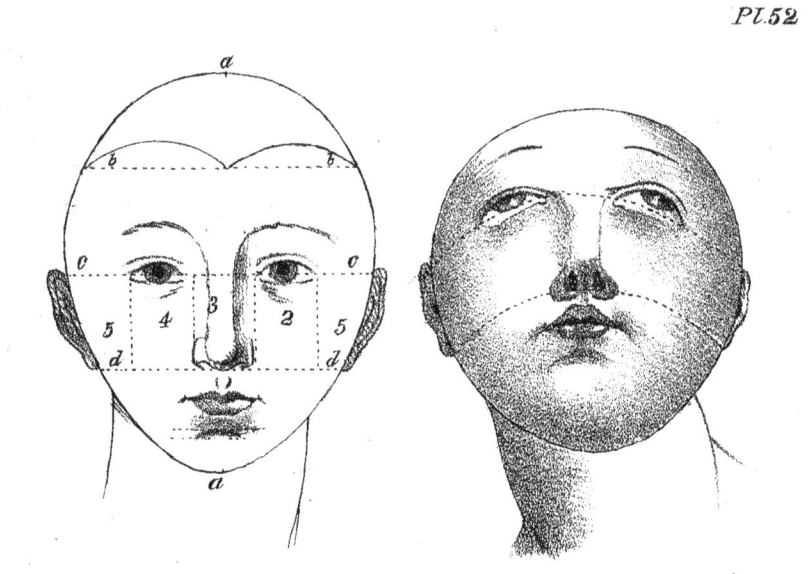

Plate LIII. Contains ovals in various directions, all marked according to the proceeding rules. No. 1. has the lines without the features. In Nos. 2. and 3. the oval is inclined to the right and left, to produce a three-quarter face; the lines still seen. Nos. 4. and 5. are head looking up and down. No. 6. is the head in profile, in which of course the line *a a*, seen in the first example in the middle of the face becomes the outline. You must here observe, that the line d d, which runs from the lowest part of the nose under the ear, always marks the termination of the back part of the head in a full grown person. To prove this turn over to No. 1. Plate LIV where I have drawn a human skull and placed on it the line by which you measure the head; you will find that the part of the skull called the occipitis terminates at the point, and the vertebræ of the neck commence. No. 2. in this plate is introduced to show you a method used by some artists of finding the place for the ear, and other features, by means of an equilateral triangle; but I cannot say that I think the rule a good one in all cases. Nos. 3. and 4. in this plate are sketches of heads without the lines, to teach you to place all the features properly without them; and here let me remind you, that having once thoroughly learned the foregoing rules for drawing the head, you must habitually call them to mind whenever you attempt to sketch a face, till they become quite familiar to you; you will then have no occasion to mark the lines on your drawings but will be able to place the features correctly without their help.

Having given these rules for drawing the human head we will now proceed to the body and limbs. Plate LV. Contains a back, front, and side view of a whole length figure; and you will observe by the numbers on the side of the plate, that the whole figure is divided into eight part; the oval of the head which we have already studied forming the first, as a well proportions human figure is supposed to be eight times the length of the head. You will see the relative proportion of the limbs to the body by studying the figures in in this plate; and it is unnecessary that I should enter into detail at present. For those who do not study anatomy, as I have before observed, this must be considered the grammar of figure drawing; and you must never omit to apply the rules laid down in this plate to any figure you intend to draw, not by actual ad-measurement on the paper or canvas, but by your eye.

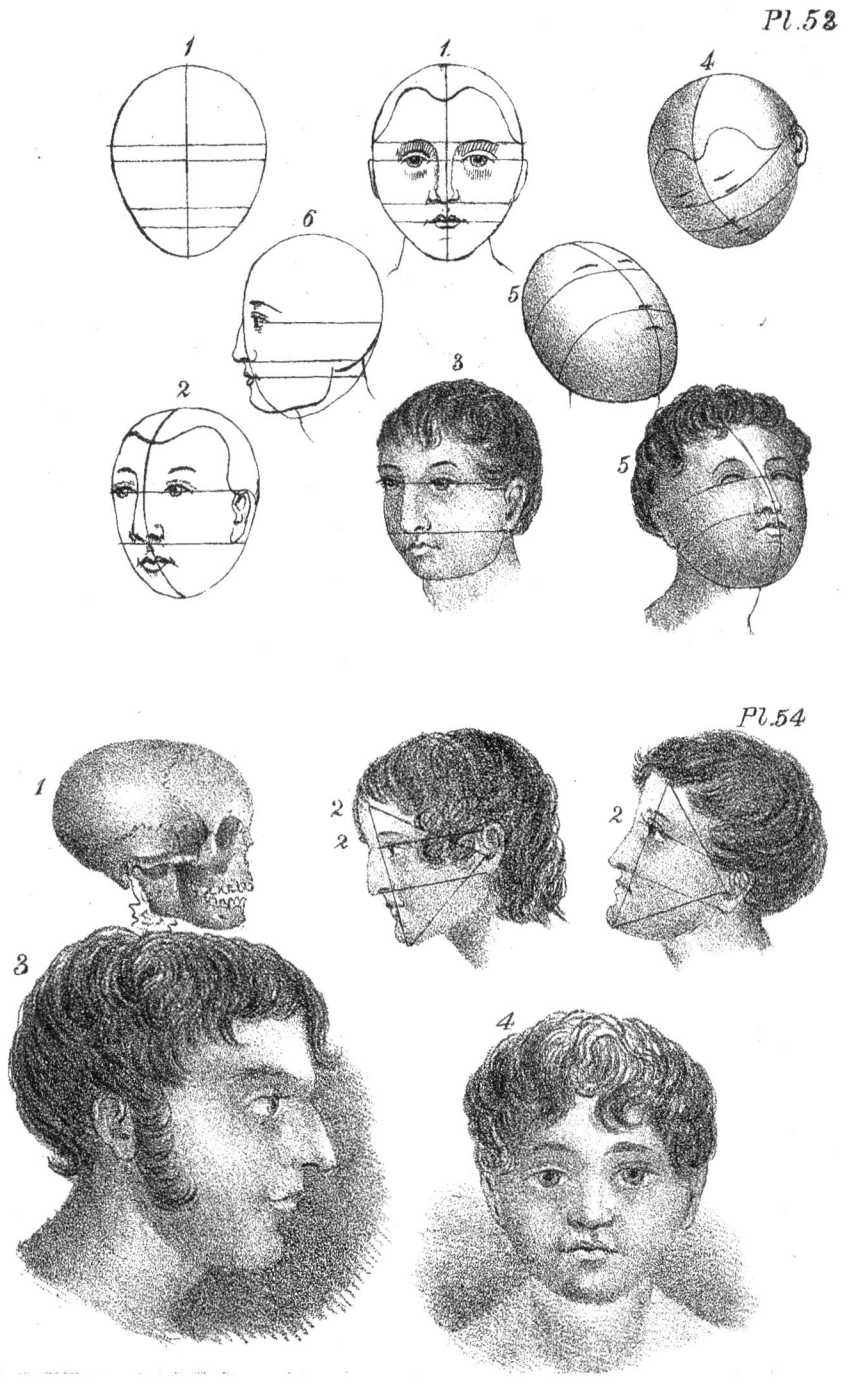

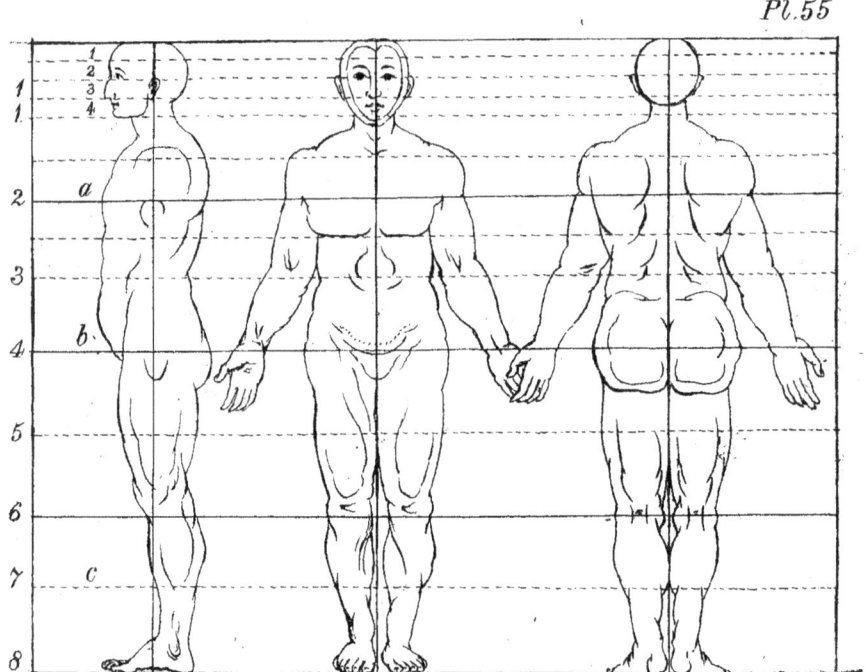

Pl.55

We must now pass on to the sketching of limbs and feature, preparatory to attempting the whole figure. You must begin with the eyes,, and they are easily drawn by any person as familiar in fronting outlines as you ought to be from your previous practice.

I have sent you in Plate LXI. six drawings of the eye in various directions: the first, you will observe, is the eye drawn directly in front. This is divided into three parts; the centre one is the size of the sight; make outlines of this eye till you can do it correctly, and then put in light and shade. Proceed in the same manner with the other four, and do not turn to another plate till you can drawn any of the eyes before you with tolerable correctness, without looking at the copy; the eye in profile is half the width of the eye in front.

Plate LIX. Contains the drawings of the nose and ears at large. No. 1. is the ear, the width of which is equal to half its height; and as we have before seen, its height is about one-quarter of the head. You must proceed as in the last plate to make outlines correctly, before you attempt a finished drawing. The nose, No. 3. is at its base. Seen in front, about the width of the eye; the other figures are too easy to require comment.

Pl. 56

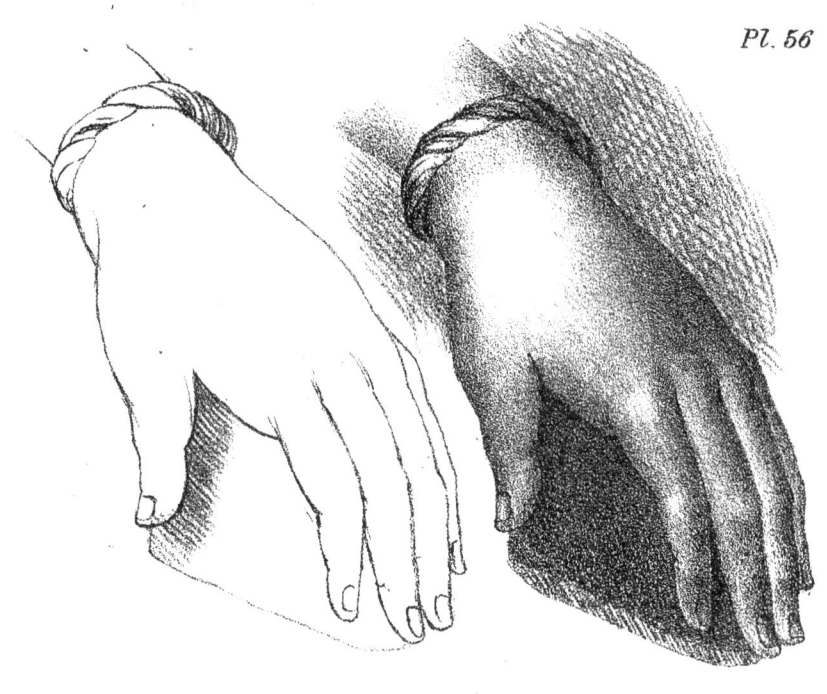

Pl. 57

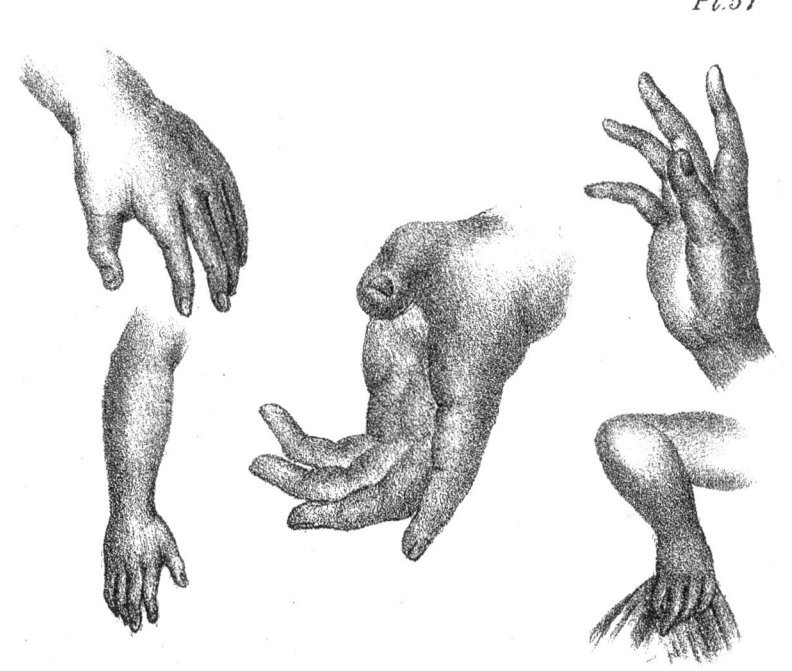

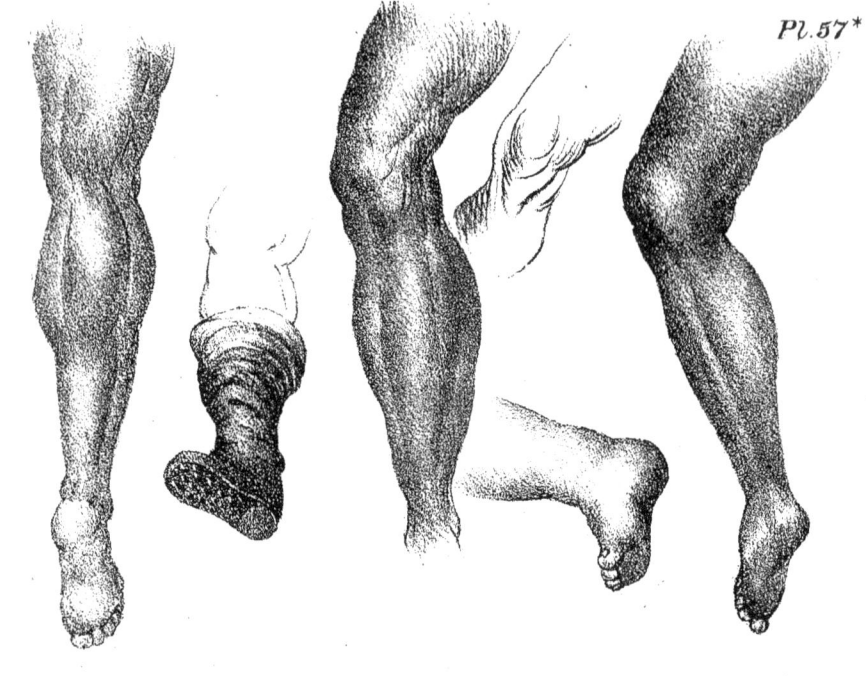

Pl. 57*

Pl. 58

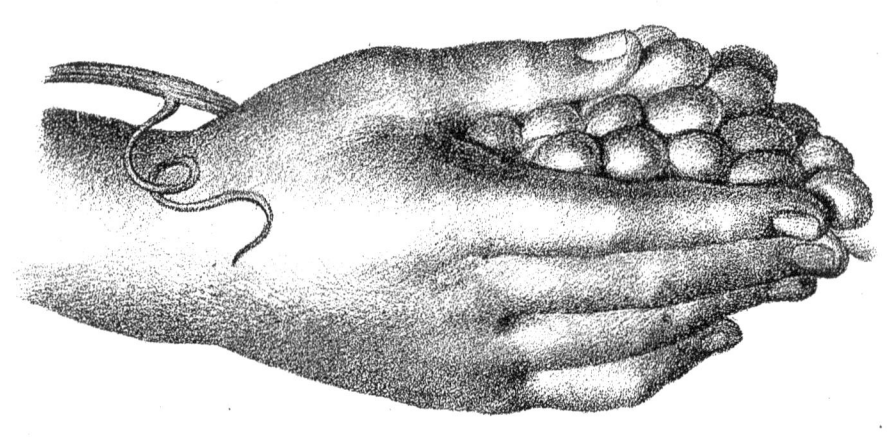

J. Collins Lith.

52

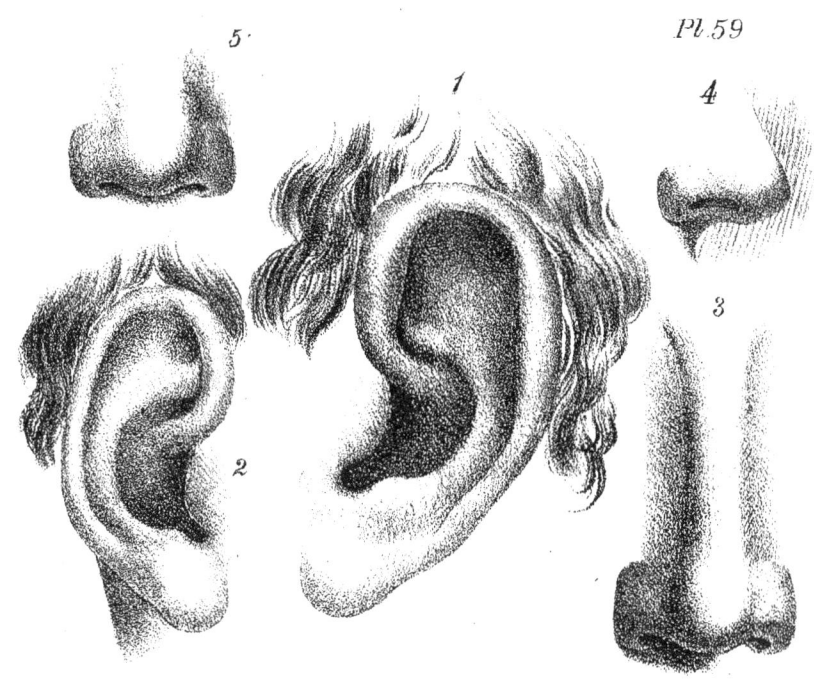

Pl. 59

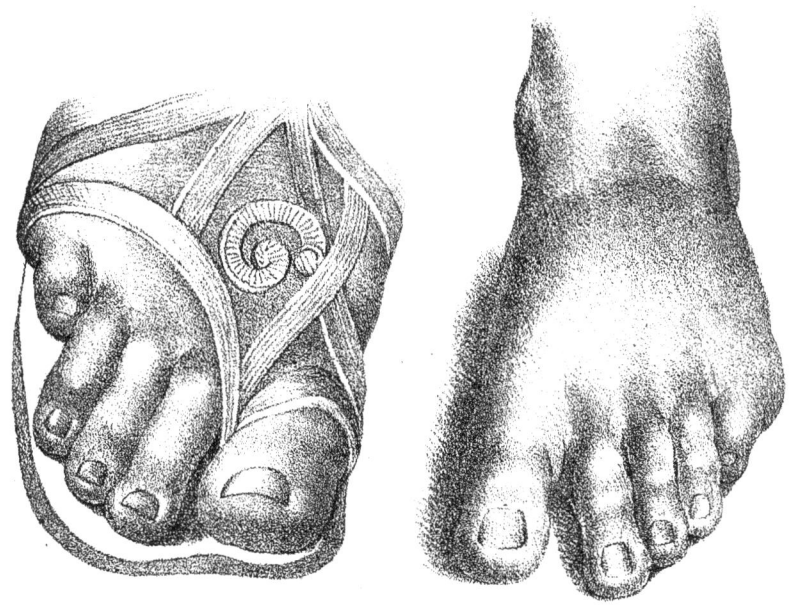

Pl. 60

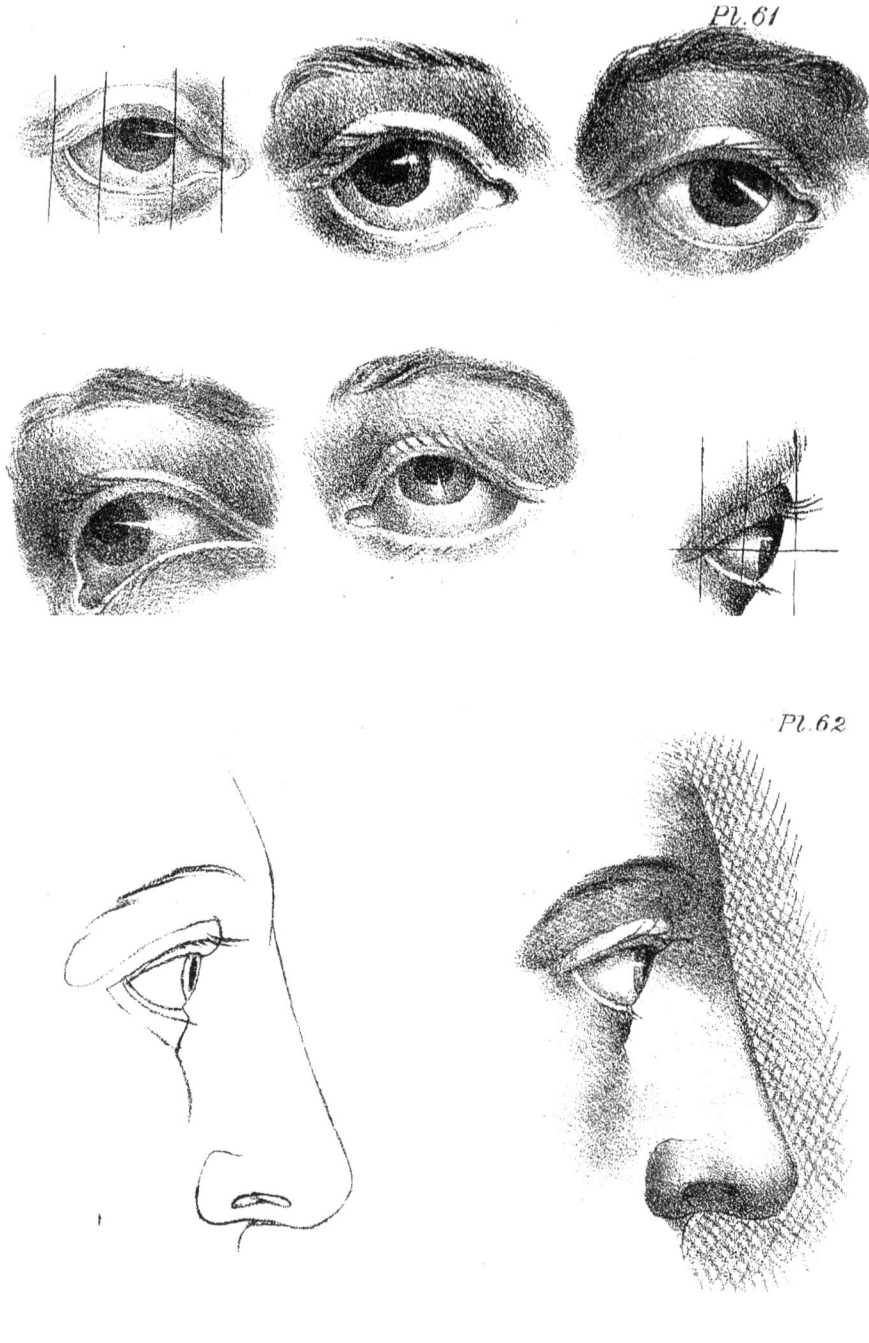

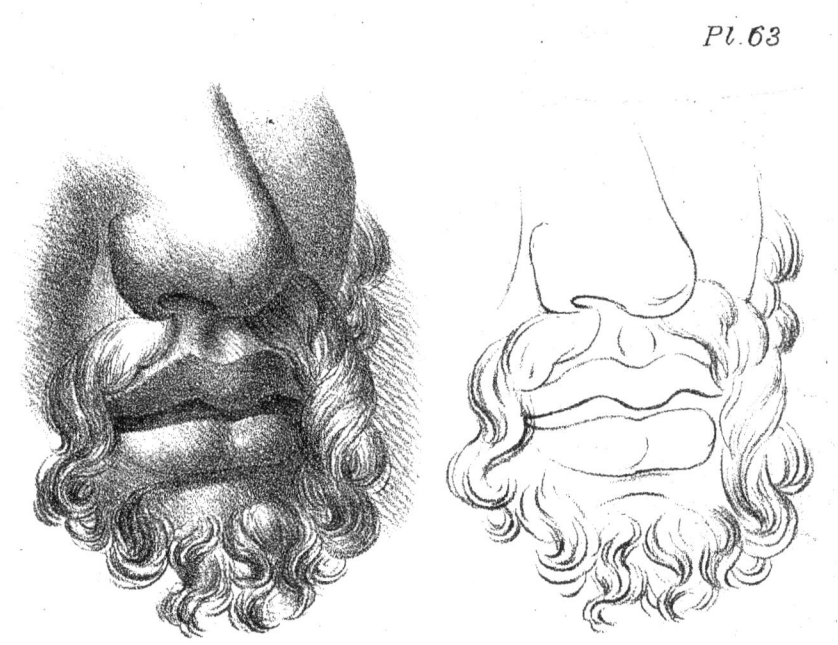

Pl. 63

PLATE LXIII. Contains a drawing of a mouth and part of the nose, from an antique figure, and as this example is more complex than any you have before attempted on this subject, I have sent both outline and finished drawing. When you can draw the eyes, nose, mouth, and ears correctly, you may proceed to combine them with other feature. The same remark will apply to Plate LXII.

Plate LVI. Contains an outline and finished drawing of a hand from the antique, and the following plates, LVII. And LVIII. Consist of hands, arms, and legs, in various directions, and one of which will form an excellent study; they are taken from the highest authority.

Plate LX. Contains a drawing of feet from the statues of the Apollo Belvedere and the Medicean Venus; these statues are supposed to be the highest standards of male and female beauty. The feet in the plate are the size of the original. In shading any of these figures, keep the hatching line clear, and cross them diagonally, so that they may form diamonds rather than squares. Do not fill any part with a close tint of the pencil or chalk, but make the shadows stronger by recrossing the lines where it is required.

LETTER X.

As you are by this time able to make correct drawings of the separate parts of the human figure, we will proceed to subjects in which they are united.

Plate LXIV. Is an outline and finished drawing of the lower part of the face seen in profile. The outline must be studied first and every part formed correctly, observing to make that part of the outline more dark and broad which will afterwards be put in strong shade. This is done in the outline before us in the touch under the nose, the lower part of the upper lip, and the corner of the mouth. This variation in the strength of the line, according to the situation, often renders free outline drawing more pleasing than elaborately finished subjects; remember it is impossible to make a good drawing, if the outline is not perfect. You may not proceed to put the sketch in the first shade, by covering all parts of the drawing, except that which is left in strong lights, with curved lines; cross these lines for the darker or second shade, taking care to hold the pencil or port-crayon as far as possible from the point, that the line may be long and free. After putting the nose and mouth in shade, lay in the back ground with line crossing each other diagonally, till you get the whole mass a shade darker than the middle tint on the face. This back ground will throw the whole mass a shade darker than the middle tint on the face. This back ground will throw the strong light left on the face very forward, and at the same time keep the dark tints from appearing too black by contrast with the white paper to which, without the back ground it would be opposed. This nice balancing of light and shade is technically called the keeping of a picture, a subject which I shall treat of more fully when we return to landscape drawing. When you have finished the back ground, give the last spirited touches to the lowest part of the nose and lips, and the drawing is complete.

Plate LXV. Contains two heads in profile. No. 1. is a pleasing study from a picture by he celebrated French artist LeBrun, who had rendered himself famous by his accurate delineations of the human figure, when under the influence of the passions. This head represents, liveliness, cheerfulness, and attention, influenced by a degree of surprise mingled with admiration. This is an easy drawing; the only part that may give you trouble is the hair: in copying the observe that all the lines by which it is formed run from one point at the crown of the head; let the lines run in curve to every part of the head, taking care to wind and turn the in imitation of the copy.

Pl. 64

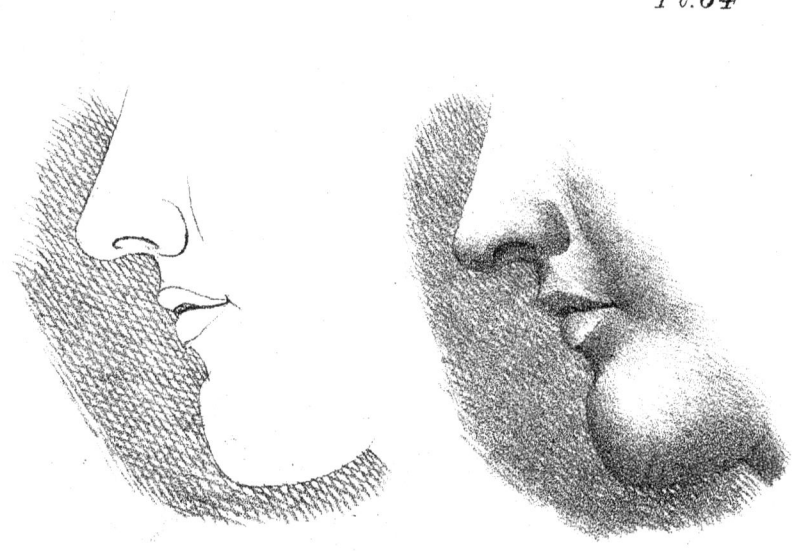

Pl. 65

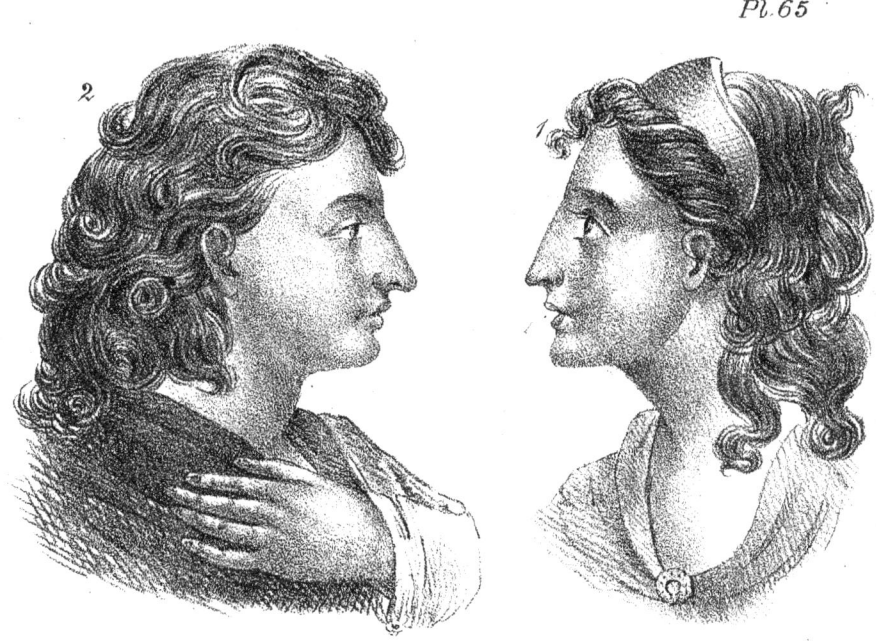

No. 2. represents respect, veneration, and admiration, expressed both by the features ad by the position of the hand on the bosom.

Pl. 66

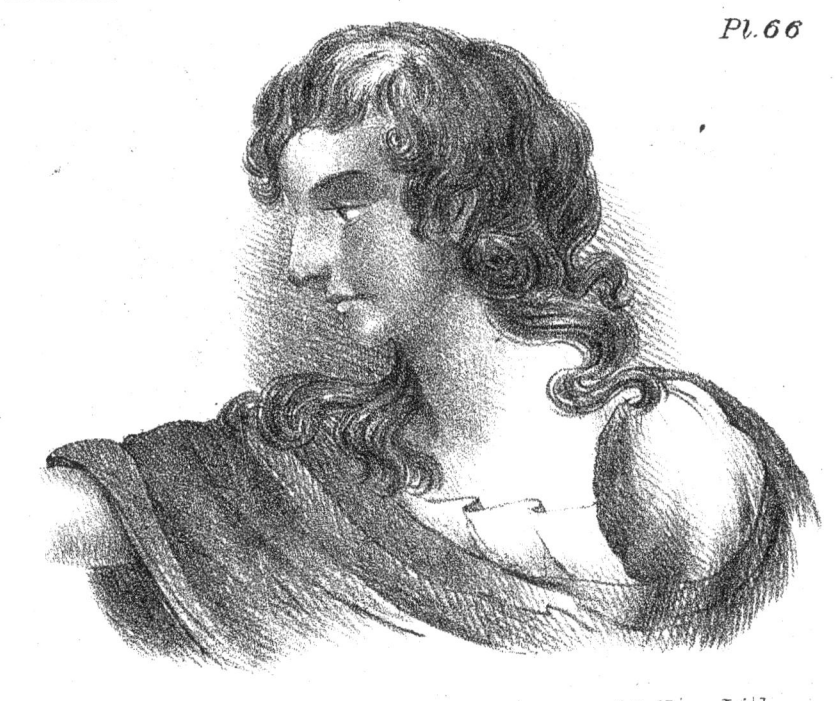

J. Collins Lith.

Plate LXVI. Is a head from a picture by Fuseli, introduced her as the last of the profiled heads that will come under our notice. The hair you observe again, all springs from one point, and terminates in wavy ringlets. The directions given for Plate LXIV. apply to the subject before us.

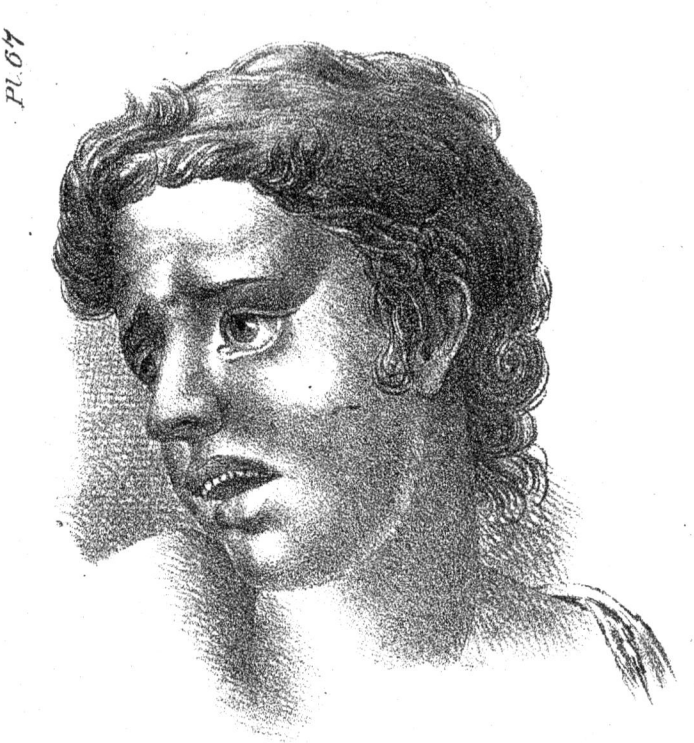

Plate LXVII. Is a fine head from the passions by LeBrun, representing bodily pain. In drawing the outline of this three-quarter face, remember the divisional lines first pointed out, as they will greatly assist you. The light, shade, and back ground, are formed as before directed, but you must take care to preserve the reflected light between the lower part of the cheek and the dark shade of the neck.

Plate LXVIII. Is a drawing from the statue of Venus de Medicis, one of the finest productions of the ancient sculptors. This head, as well as Plate LXVII. Is drawn with red chalk, which will work with as much ease as the pencil or black crayon, if you procure the best French chalk, and take care the it is soft and pleasant to the touch.

When you can copy the foregoing example correctly, it will be proper to commence the whole figure; and for that purpose, we must refer to Plate XLIV. The forester's boy and his dog. Here the division of the figure according to the rules laid down in Plate LV. Will apply. The finishing of the drawing after you have formed the outline correctly, will be easy. In small figure, like that before us, the less hatching there is on the face, the better. You must keep the hands free, and observe that the shadows thrown on the figure are all formed by lines crossing each other. The sleeping shepherd, Plate XLV. And the girl at the Spring, Plate XLVI. Are drawn by the same rule. The landscapes to both these subjects are interesting, and care must be taken that they do not overpower the principal figures. You will observe that juvenile faces are marked by peculiar roundness of form, and that the outlines of the head approaches nearer the circle than the oval.

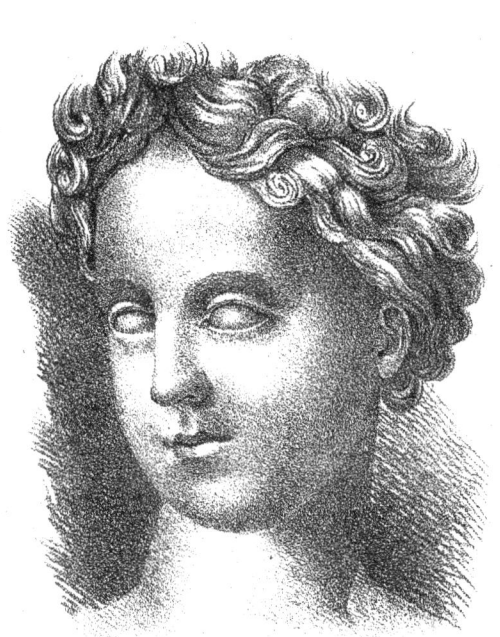

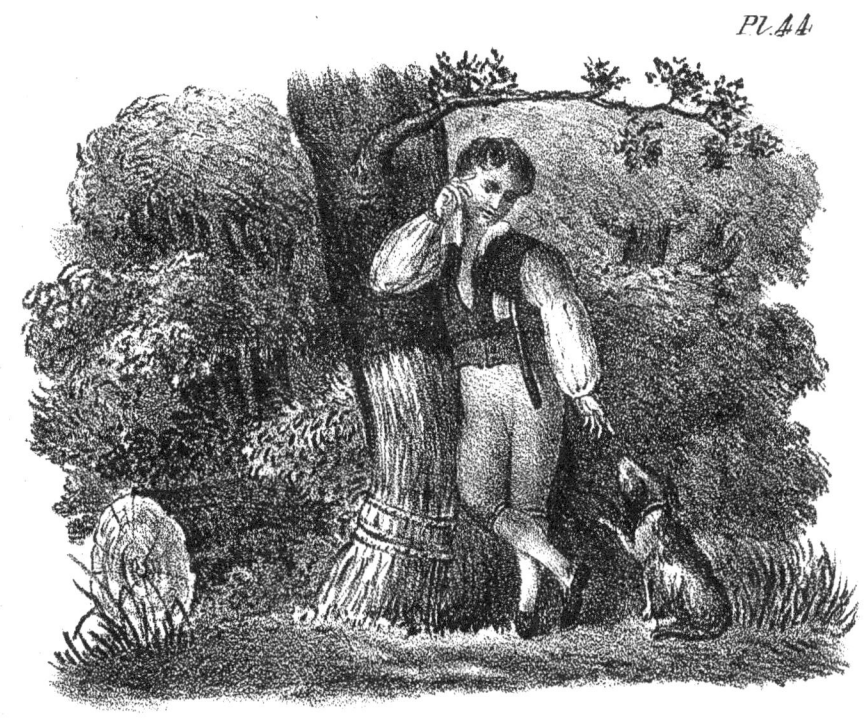

59

Pl. 45

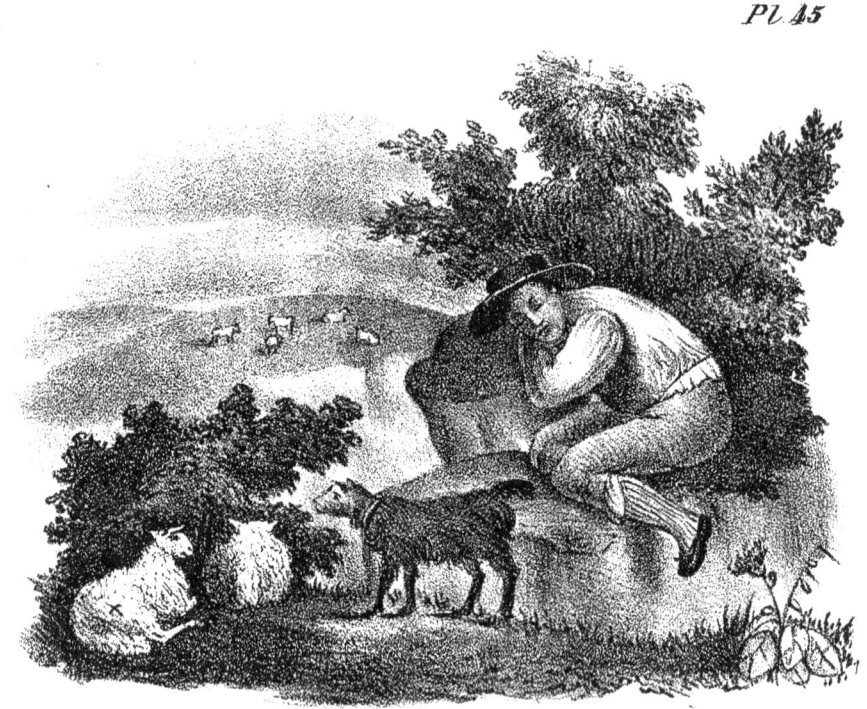

Pl. 46

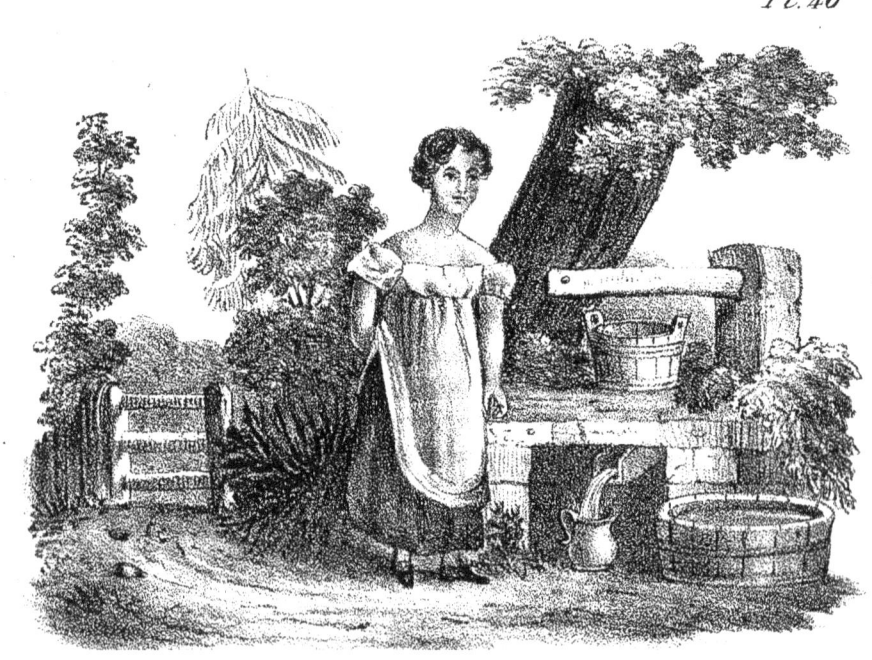

Plate LXIX. Is the statue of Apollo, which is allowed to be the finest single figure in the world, and is justly the object of universal admiration, from the elegant symmetry of every part, which gives dignity to the whole. Apollo is supposed to have just discharged his arrow at the Python. In drawing this beautiful figure, great care must be taken that the outline is flowing and correct, and that every part is firmly yet delicately shaded. When you can draw this figure, you must proceed to sketch from figures in plaster of Paris, cast from models from the antique. You will be at no loss how to proceed in placing them on paper, if you constantly refer to our early directions. When you draw from plaster figure, you must take care to let the light fall upon them from the top of the room; thus if you draw in a room that has two windows, you should close one entirely, and the other all but about one-third from the top: by this means, the figure will be in strong light and shade, and you will be able to produce the whole with force and truth, which would not be the case if the shadows were weakened by lights coming from different directions.

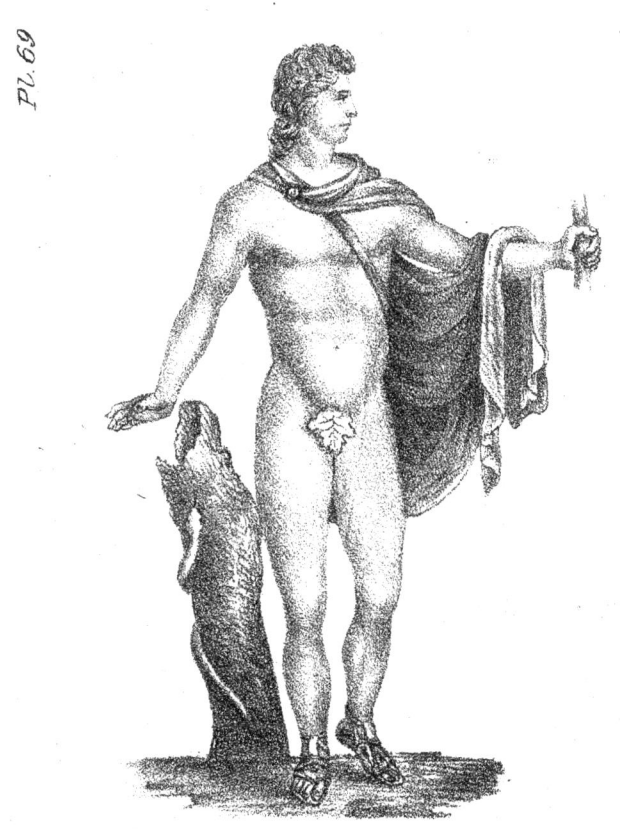

As the concluding subject on this branch of the art, I have sent you in Plate LXX. Two figures in outline with the muscles violently excited, displaying themselves with great force. These specimens will prove to you the necessity of understanding the anatomy of the exterior muscles of the body, if you intend pursuing your studies of the human figure to a greater extent than I have gone in the treatise.

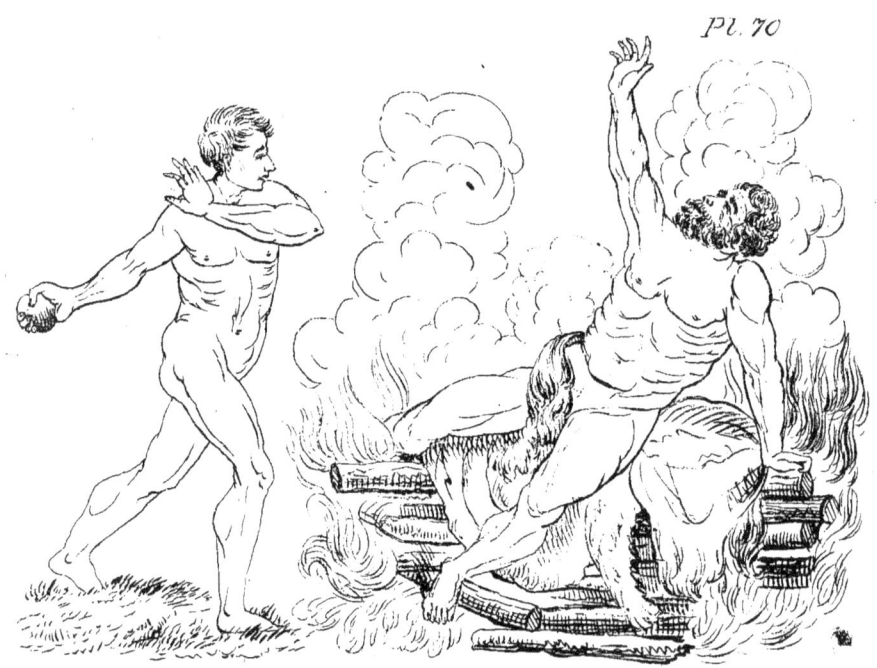

Pl. 70

The figure on the burning pile, whose writhing muscles show the acute torture he is suffering, is taken from a picture by Guido Rheni, and forms the subject of one of the four celebrated paintings by the artist of the life of Hercules. It represents the hero himself, who having discovered the centaur Nessus' plan of carrying off Dejanira, shot him with a poisoned arrow. Nessus, on the point of expiring, gave Dejanira a tonic stained with his blood, assuring her it possessed the virtue of bringing Hercules back to her if ever he should prove faithless. This garment was poisoned, and Hercules had no sooner put it on the he felt indescribable torments. He terminated them by putting an end to his life, and the god of strength and courage expired on a burning pile raised by himself.

Guido Rheni was the son of a musician, who intended him for his own profession, but the genius of Guido displaying itself early, he was placed under the direction of Dennis Calvart, a Flemish painter. He afterwards entered the school of the Caracci, and soon distinguished himself by his works, which at length attracted the attention of Pope Paul the Fifth, who took great pleasure in seeing him paint; the Prince of Tuscany and others who loaded him with presents and proofs of their esteem. Guido, endowed with an astonishing facility might have ended his days in the midst of fame and fortune, if in his later years his passion for gaming had not disturbed his working. This, added to the losses he sustained, absorbed all the fruits of his labour. Compelled to work with rapidity, he had the mortification in his old age to see his paintings little esteemed by connoisseurs: at last, pursued by creditors and abandoned by his former friends, he died in great poverty in the year 1642, aged 67.

Drawing Lessons for Family and School
John Weik, Publisher

John Weik published a series of 73 small 6 page pamphlets which he advertised saying "Each Number contains 6 plates in cover. All the branches of which a complete drawing school ought to comprise are contained in this series. Every branch is by a thorough tutor in drawing systematically arranged, and the whole affords the best qualities of becoming a part of every school library." And "Each Number contains 6 plates, put up as drawing-books with excellent drawing cards opposite to each drawing. This saves the scholar from baying a drawing book and prevent confusion or loss of his drawing cards." These were published around 1855.

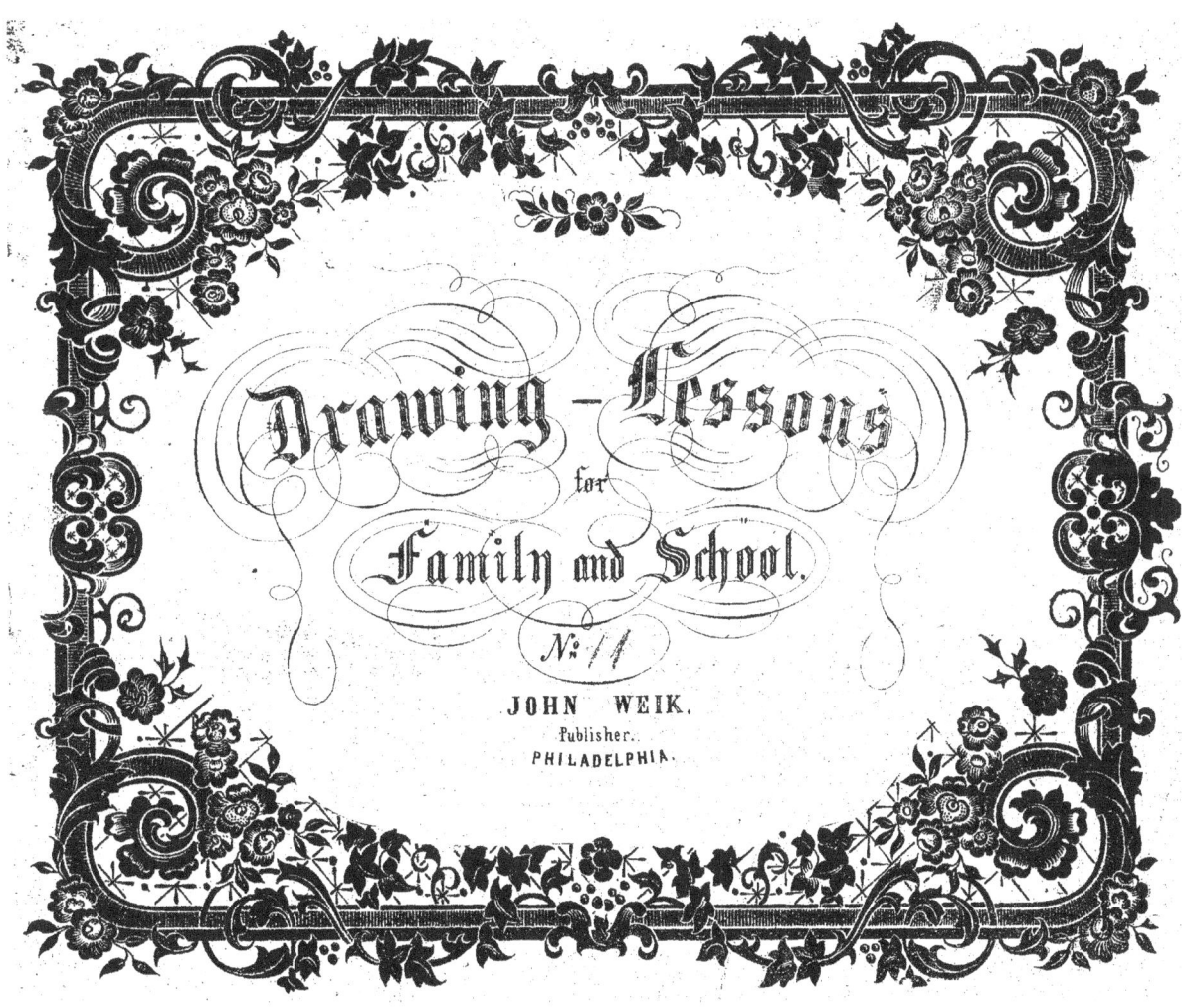

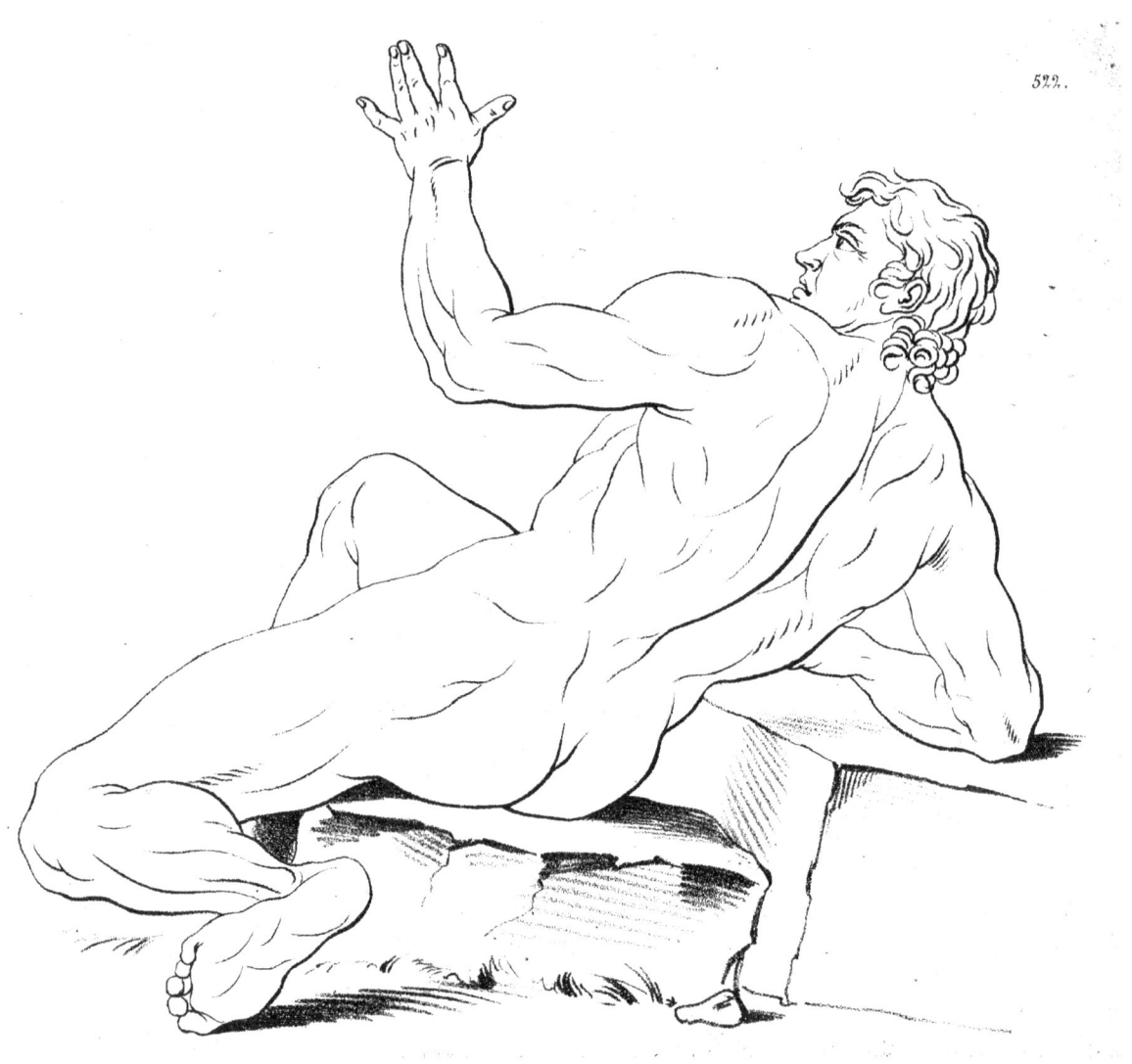

522.

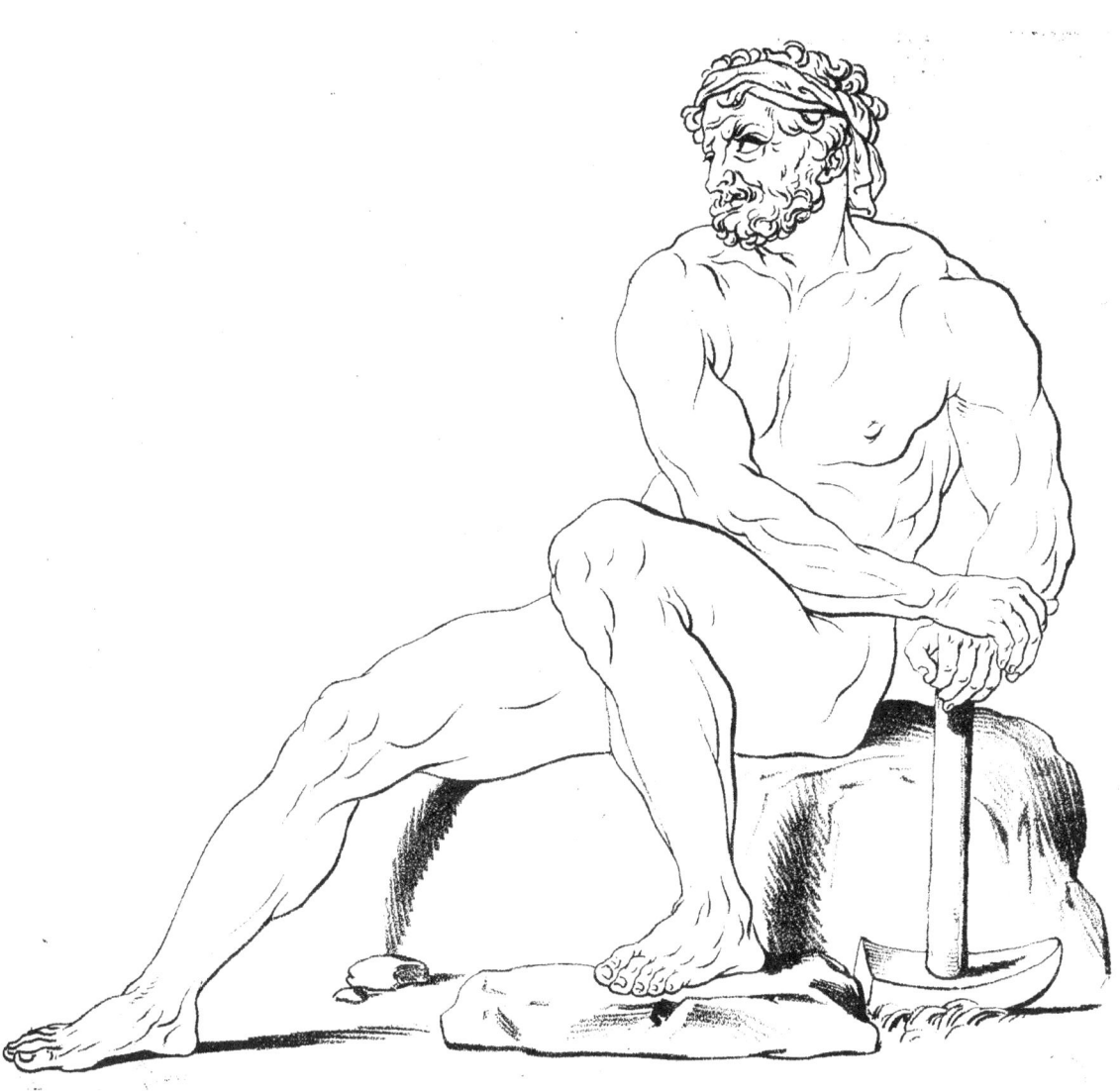

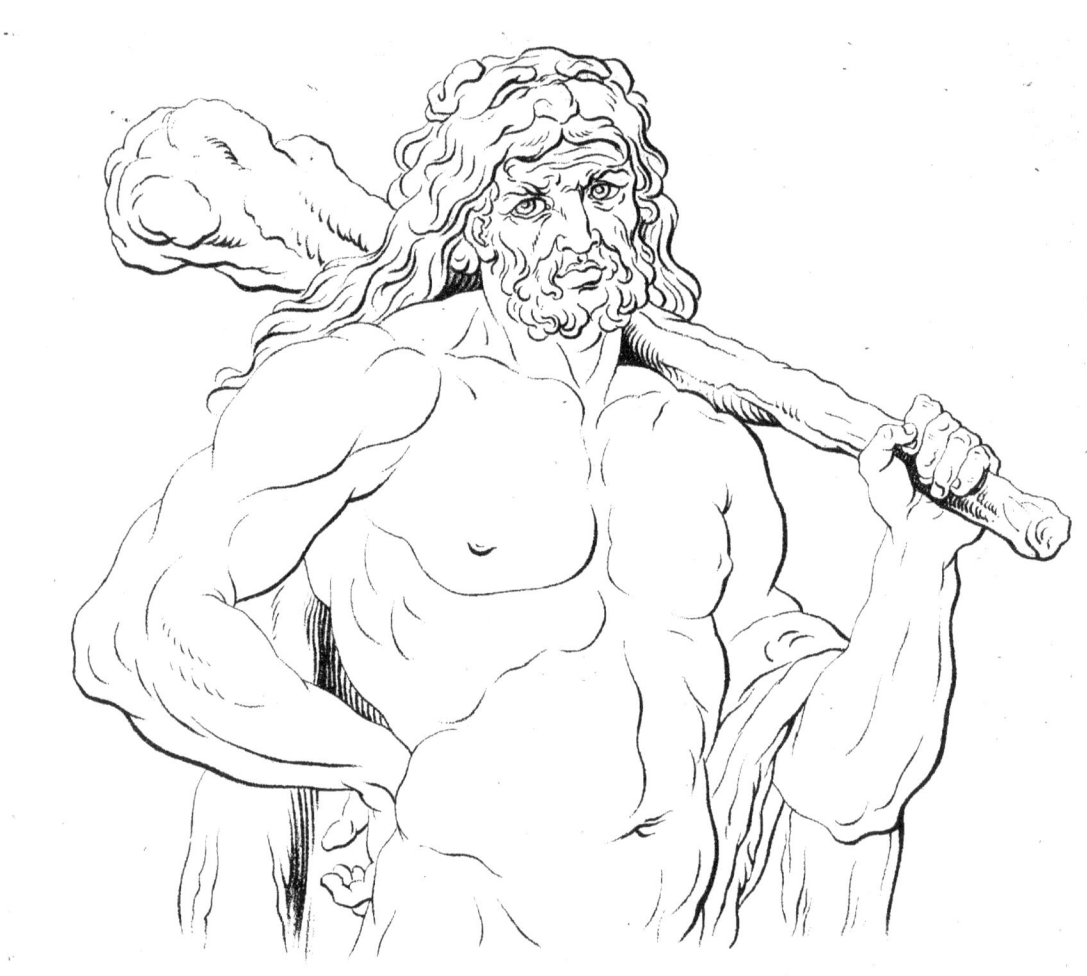

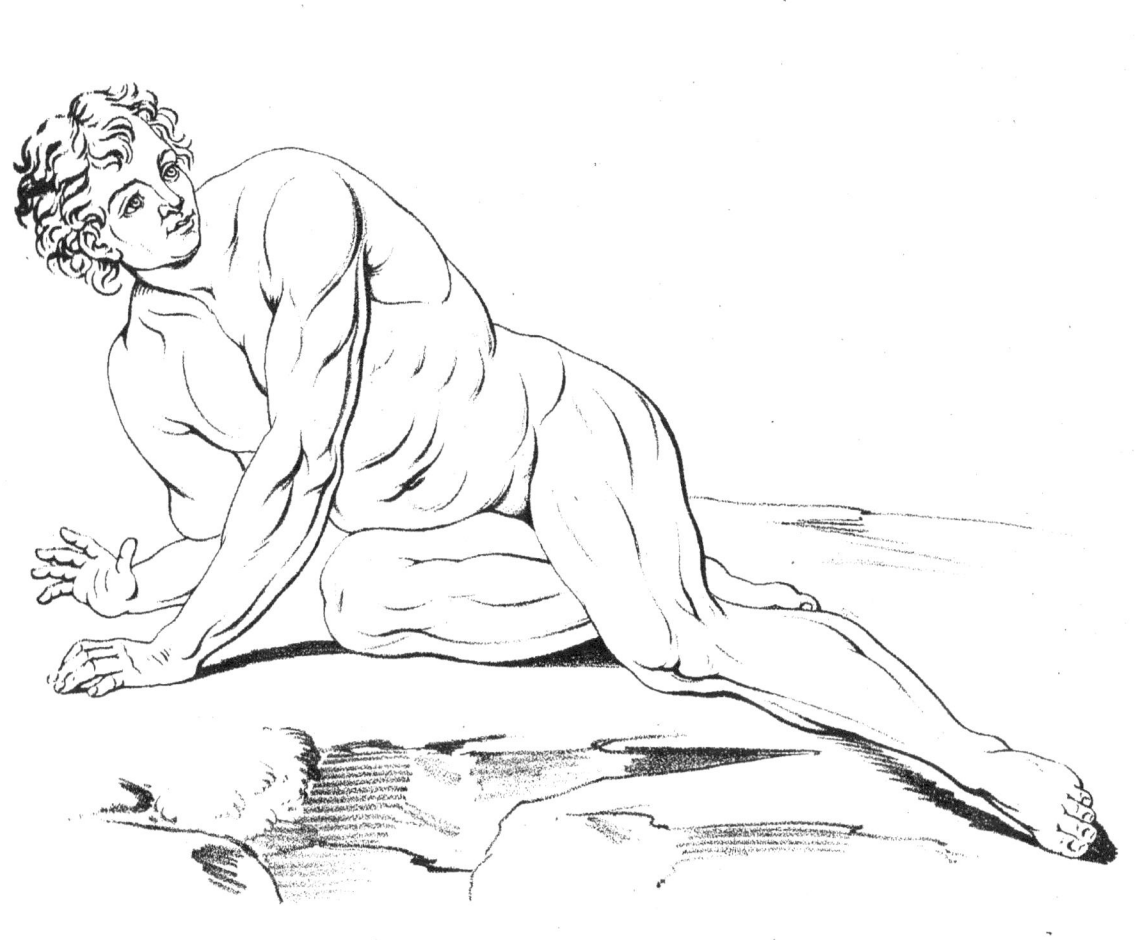

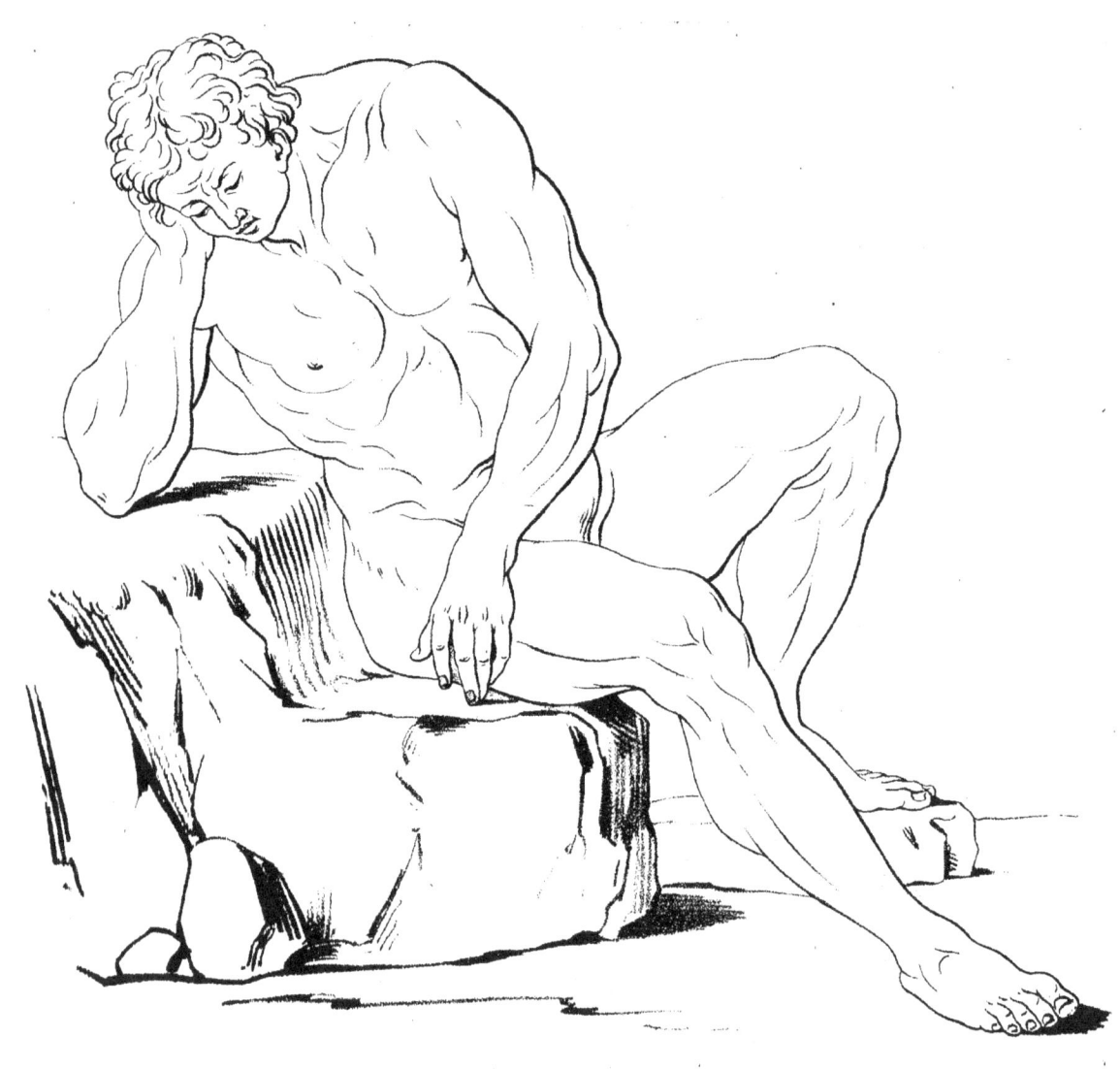

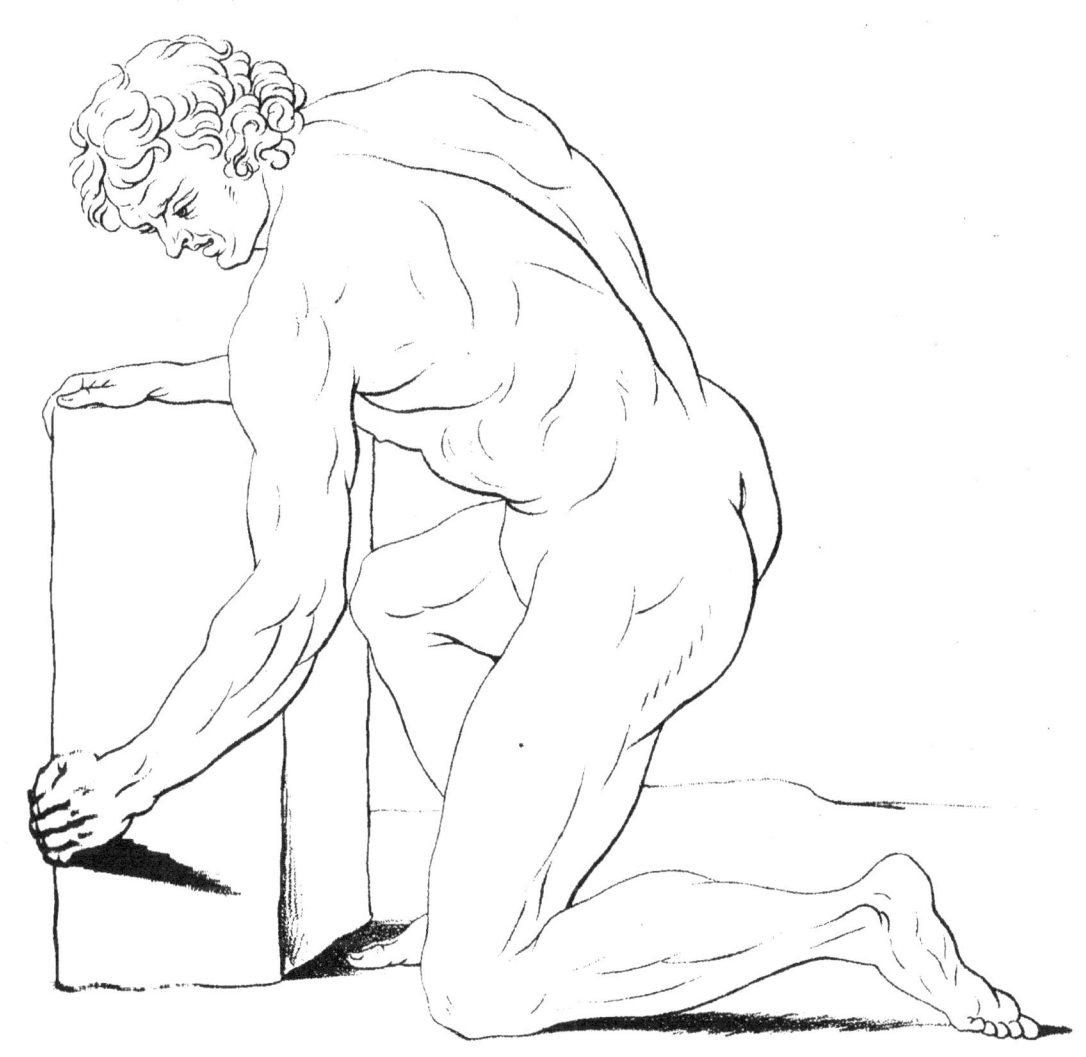

Wilhelm Hermes
Berliner
Systematische Zeichen Schule
für
Lehrer und zum Selbst-Unterricht

Wilhelm Hermes *Systematic Drawing School for Teachers and self-teaching* was a popular copy book both in Germany and in translation in Great Britain and the United States. It consisted of a series of booklets that were published between 1853 and 1855. The course was called Wilhelm Hermes' United States Systematic Drawing School in the United States. And was published around 1862.

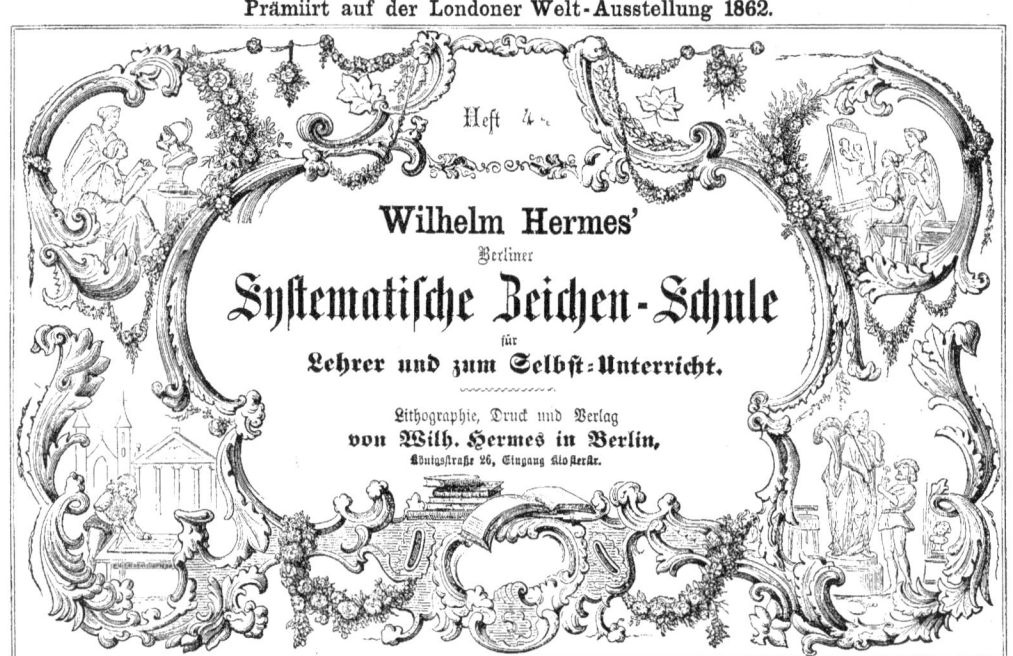

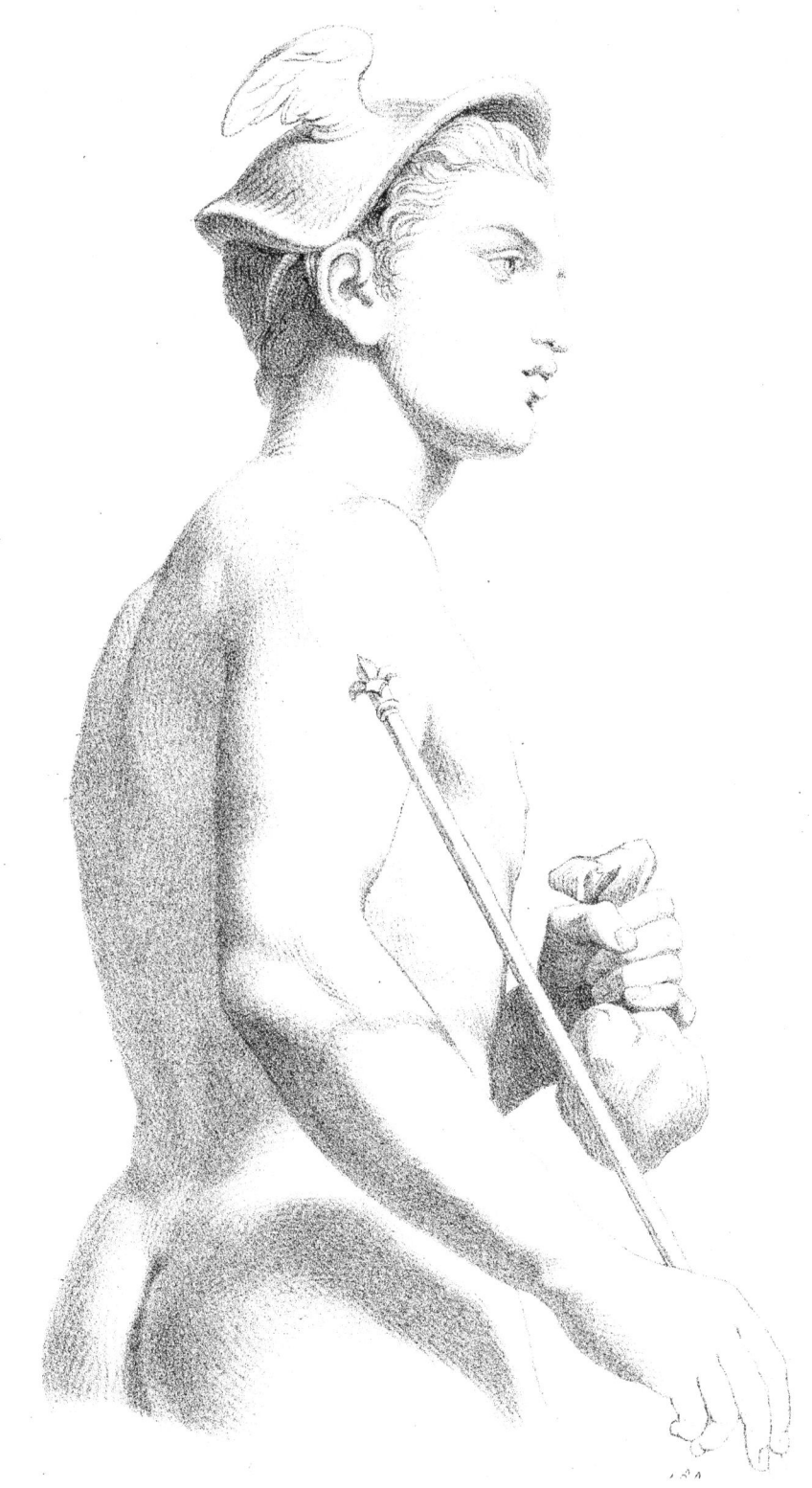

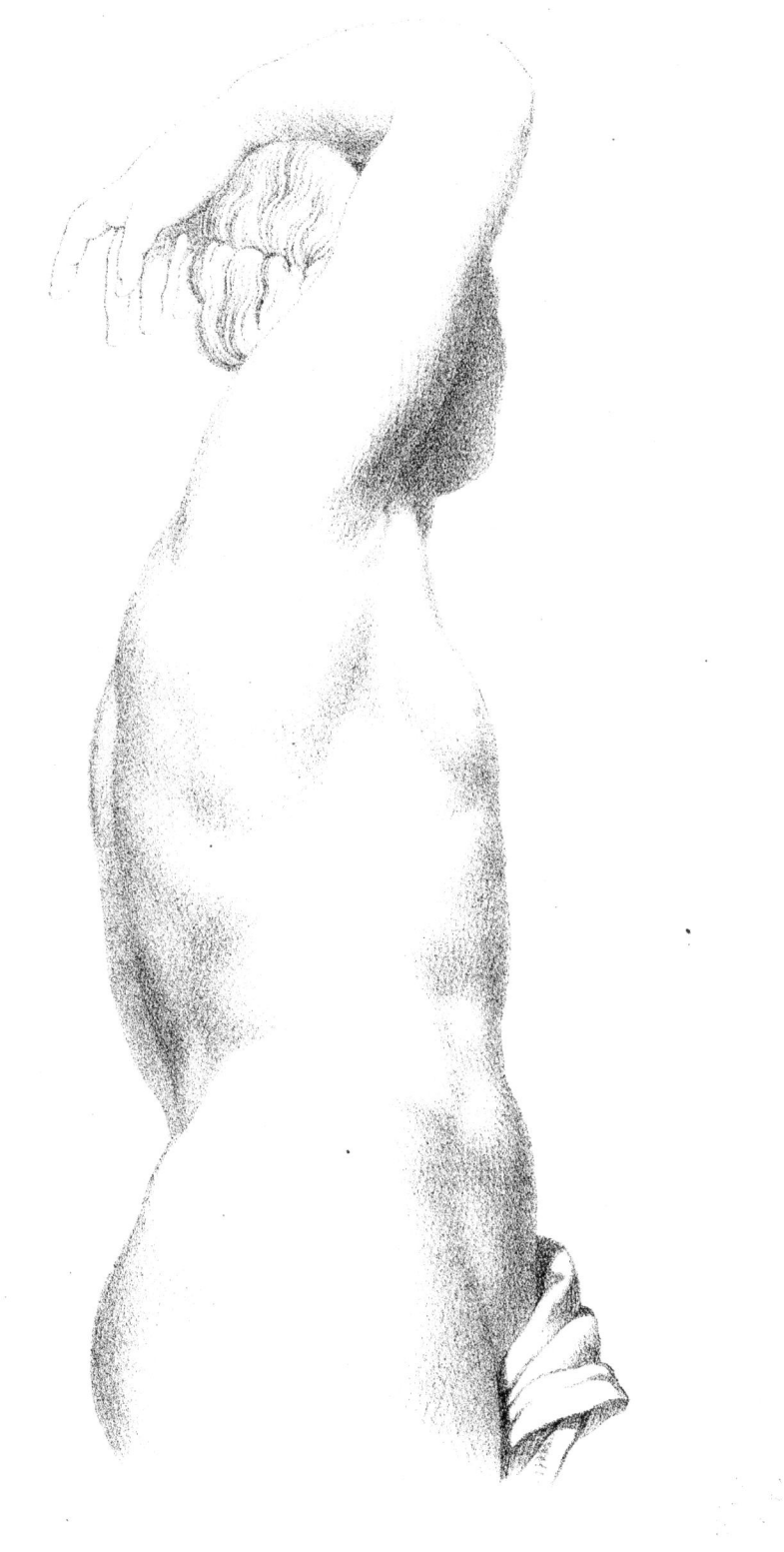

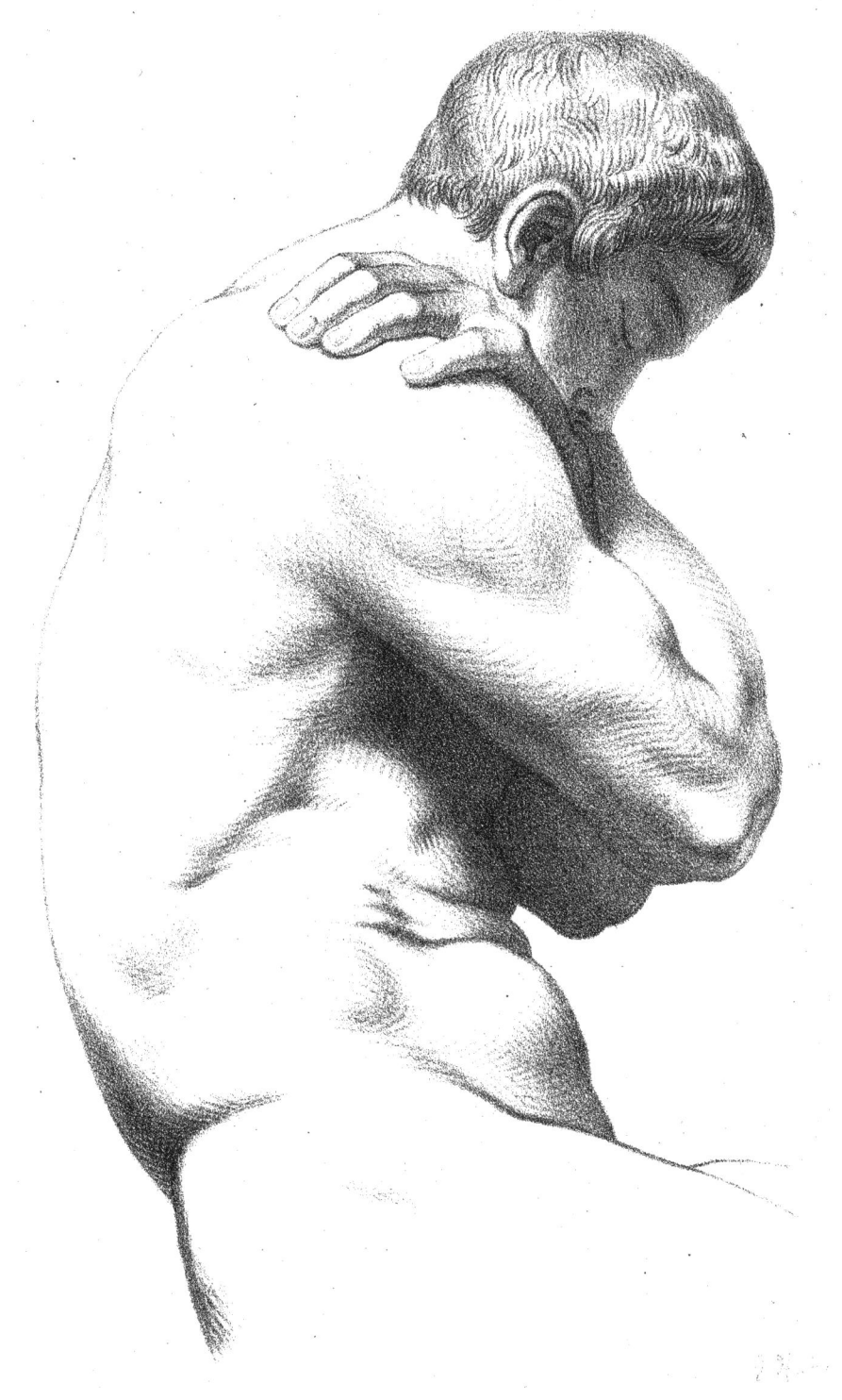

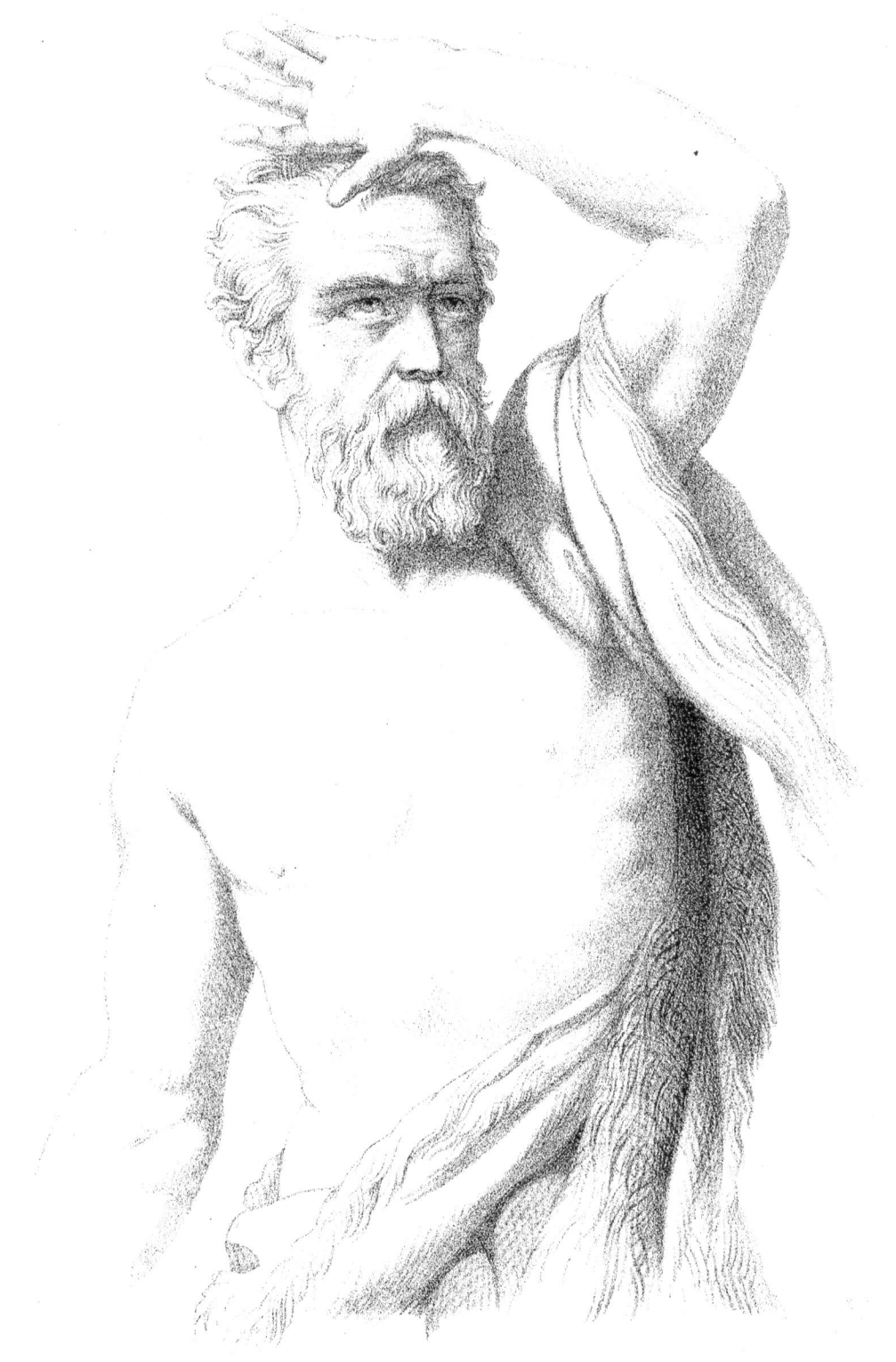

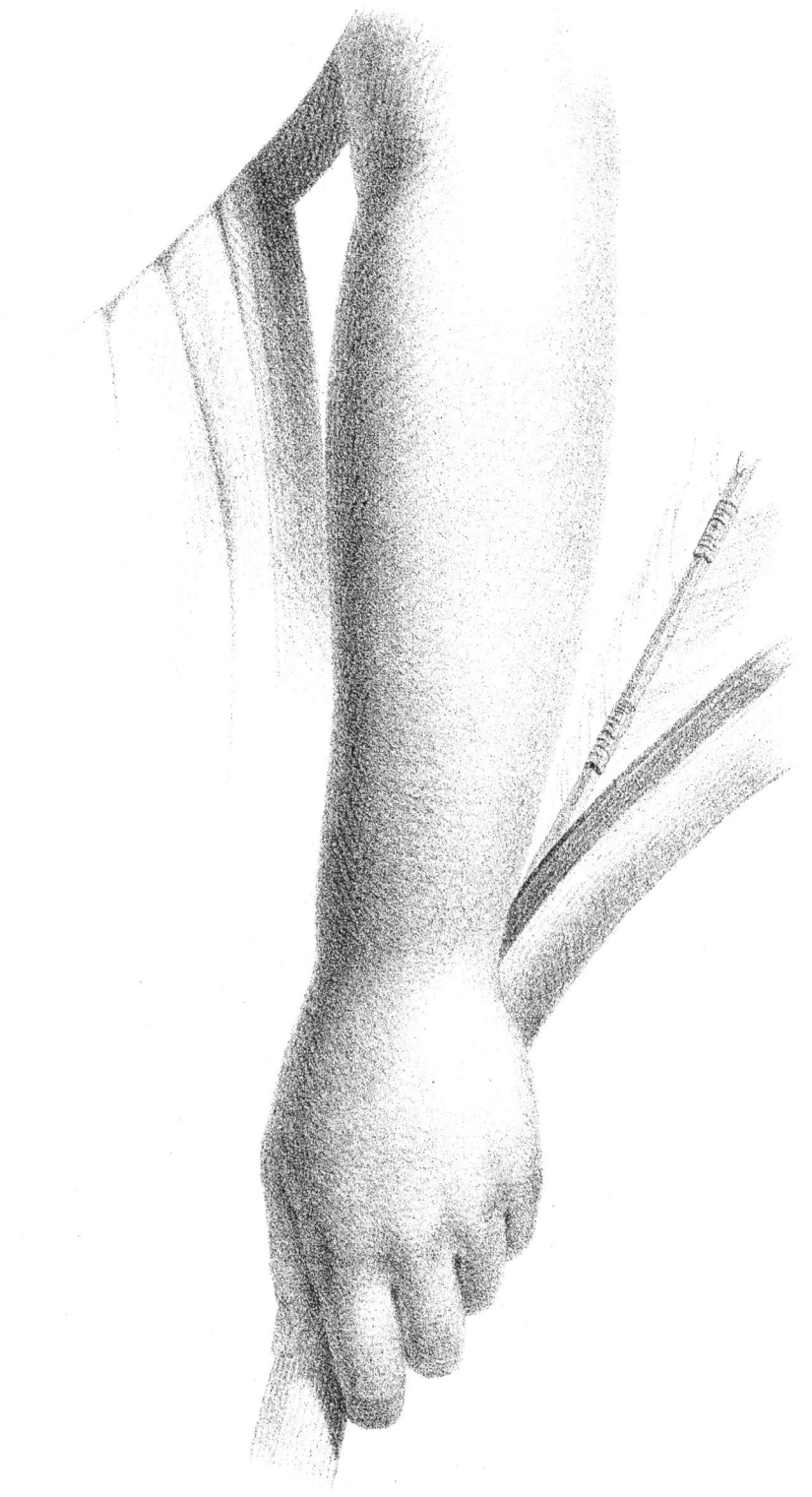

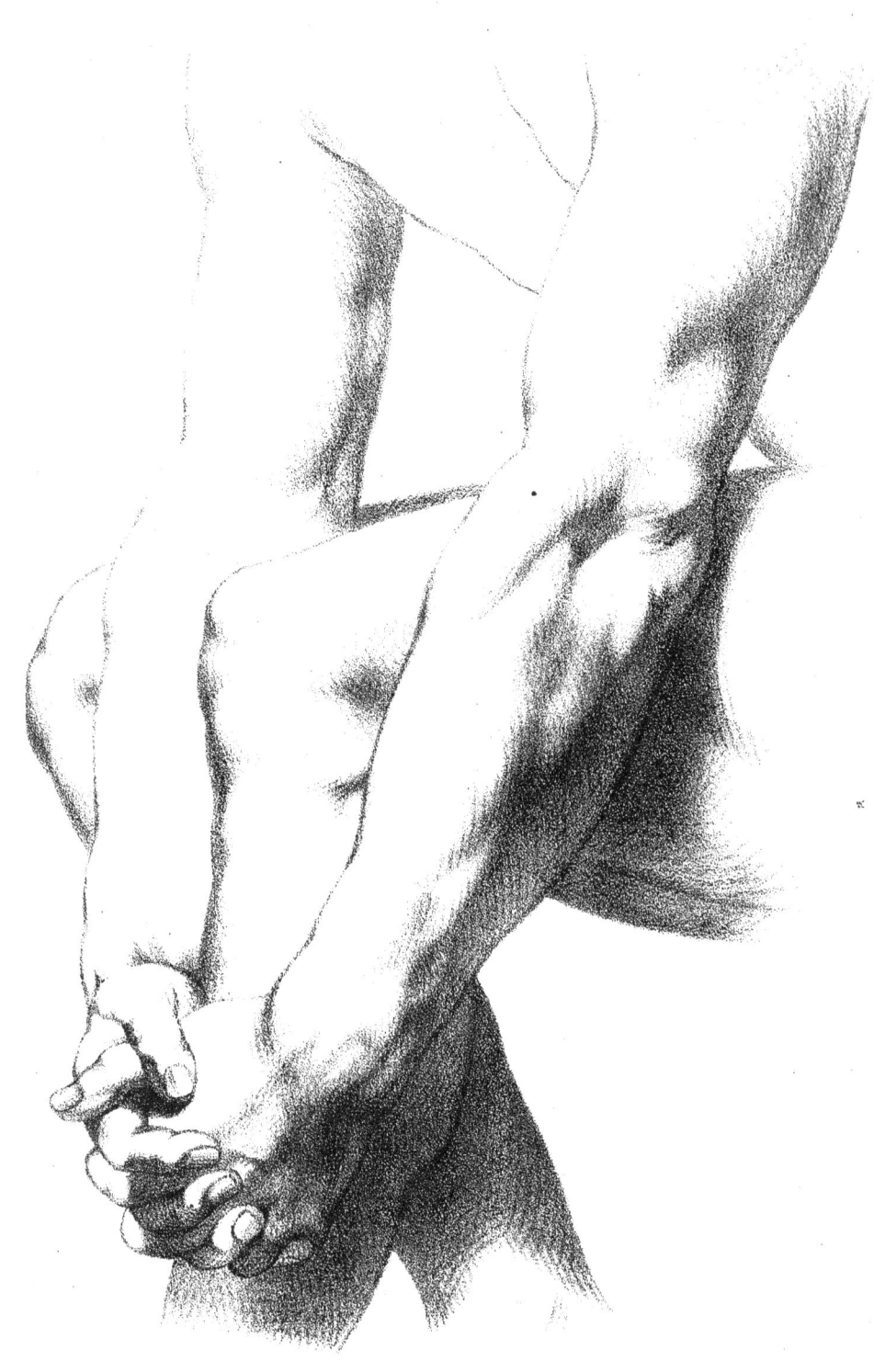

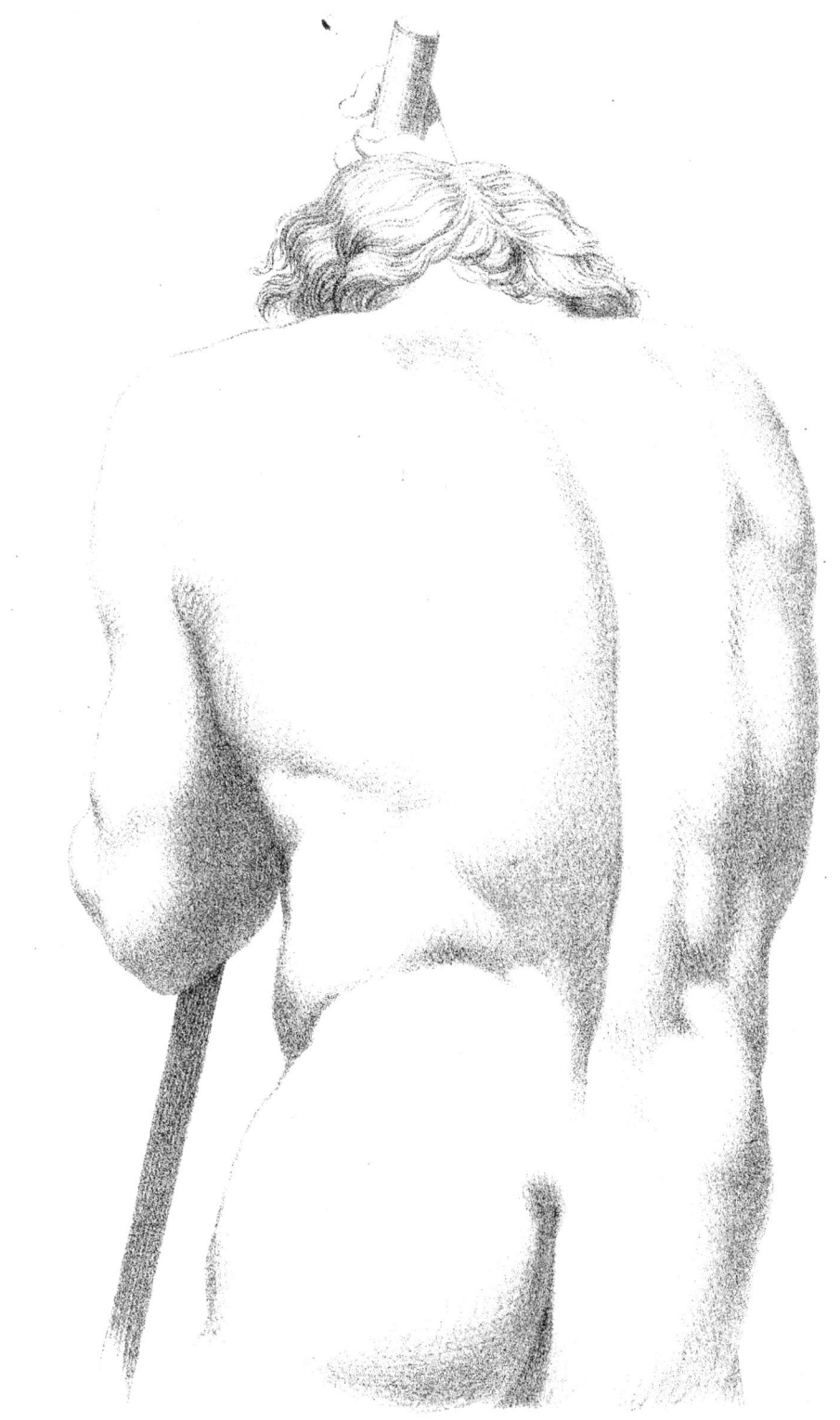

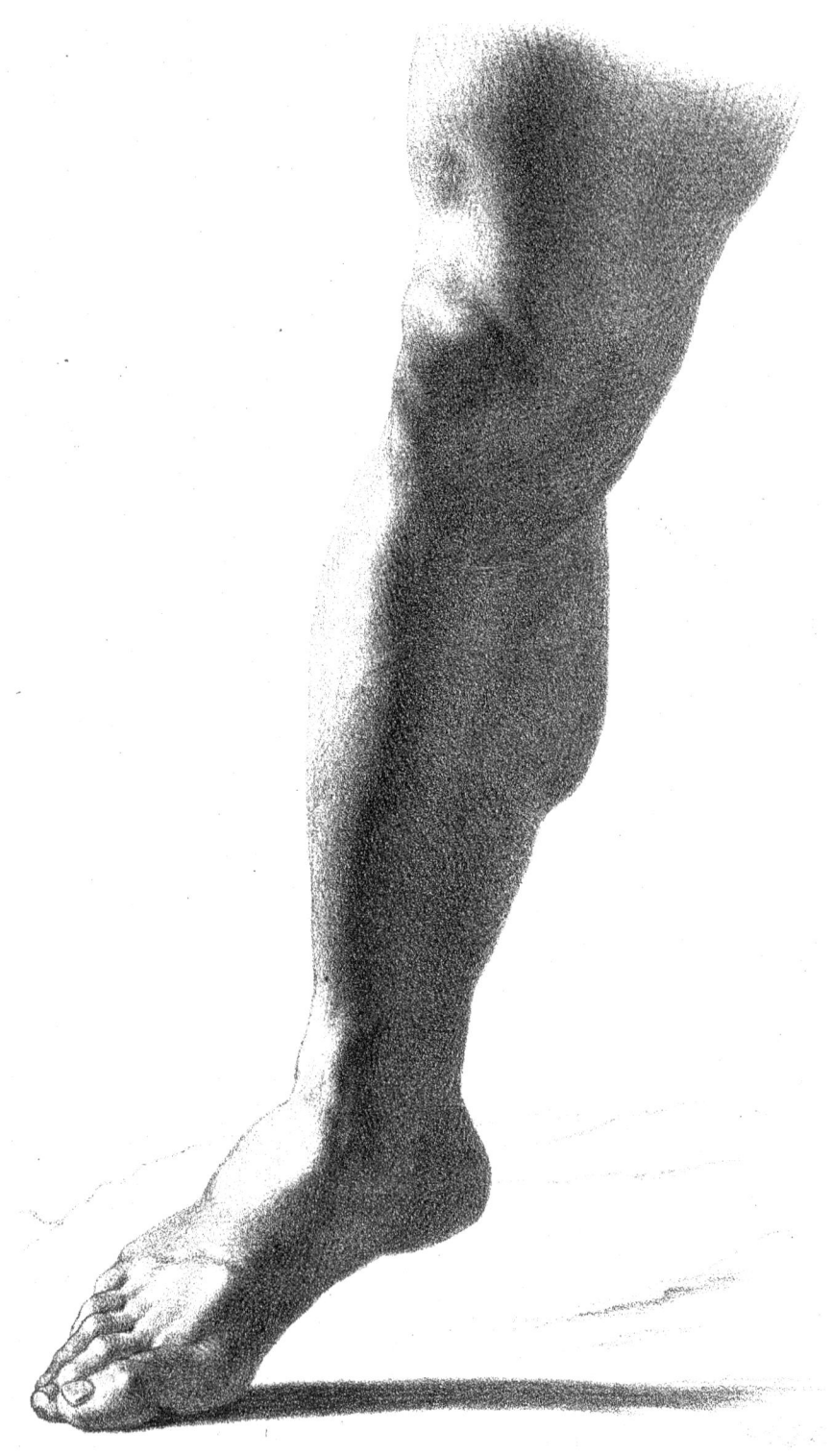

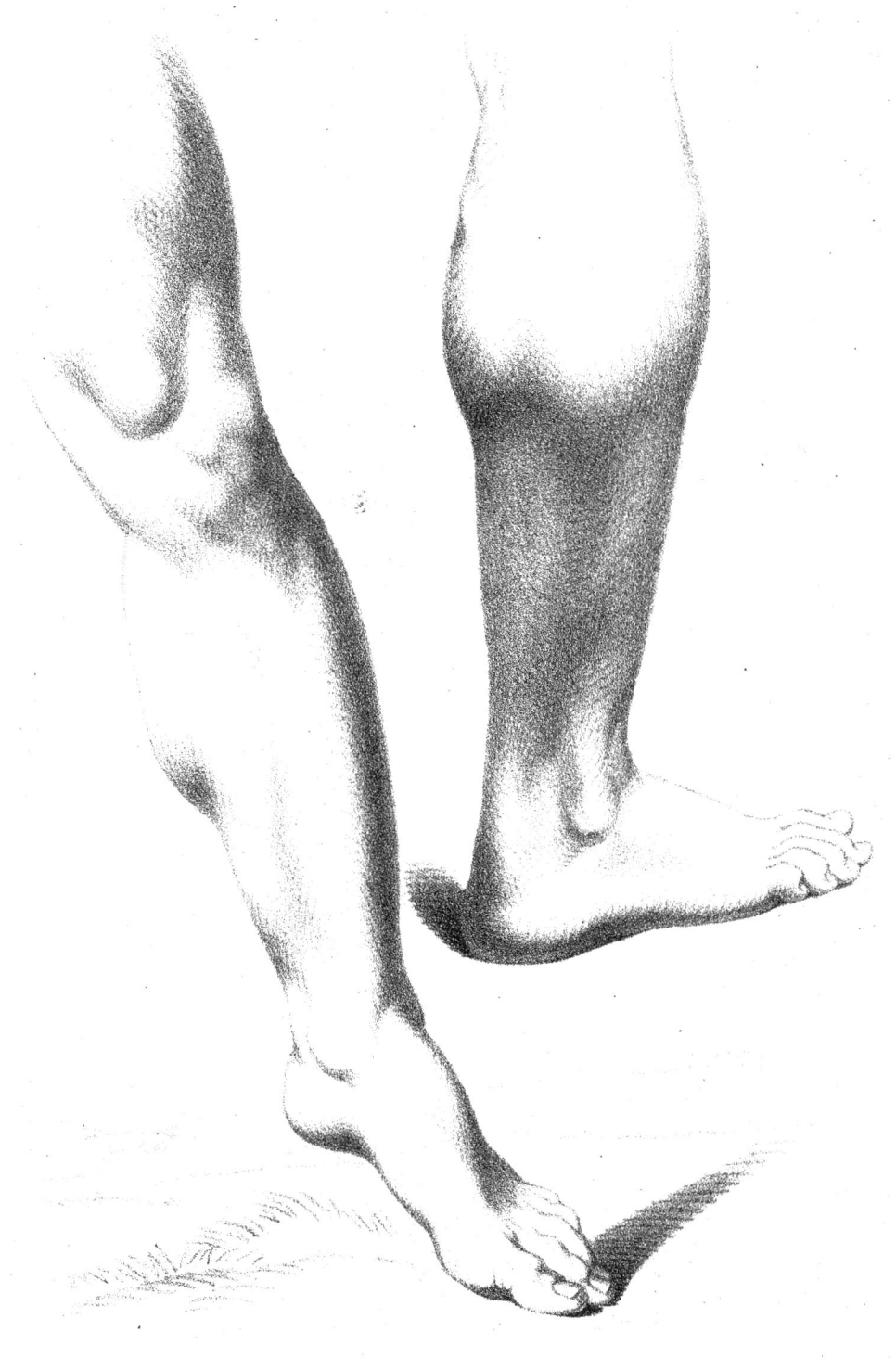

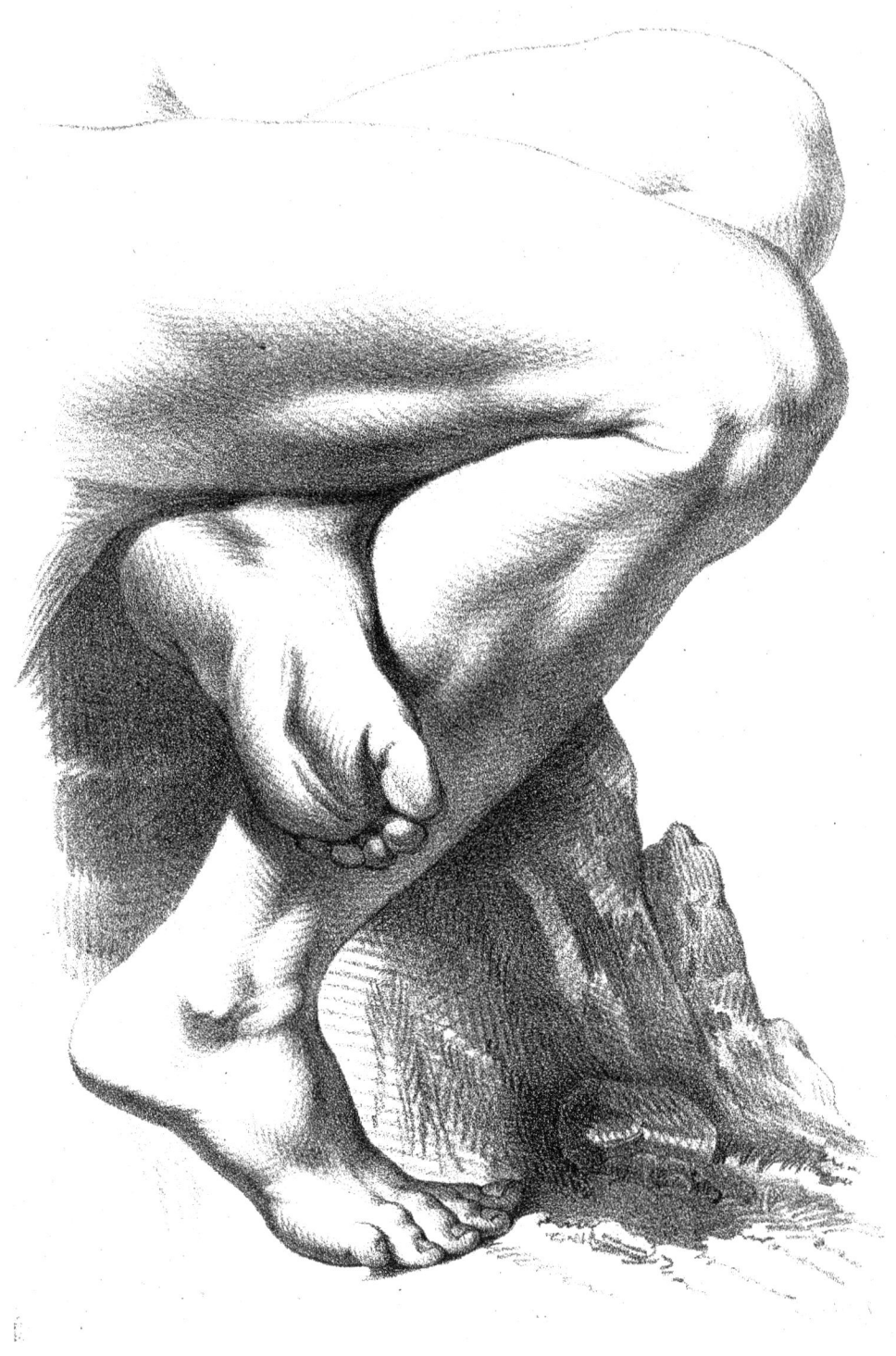

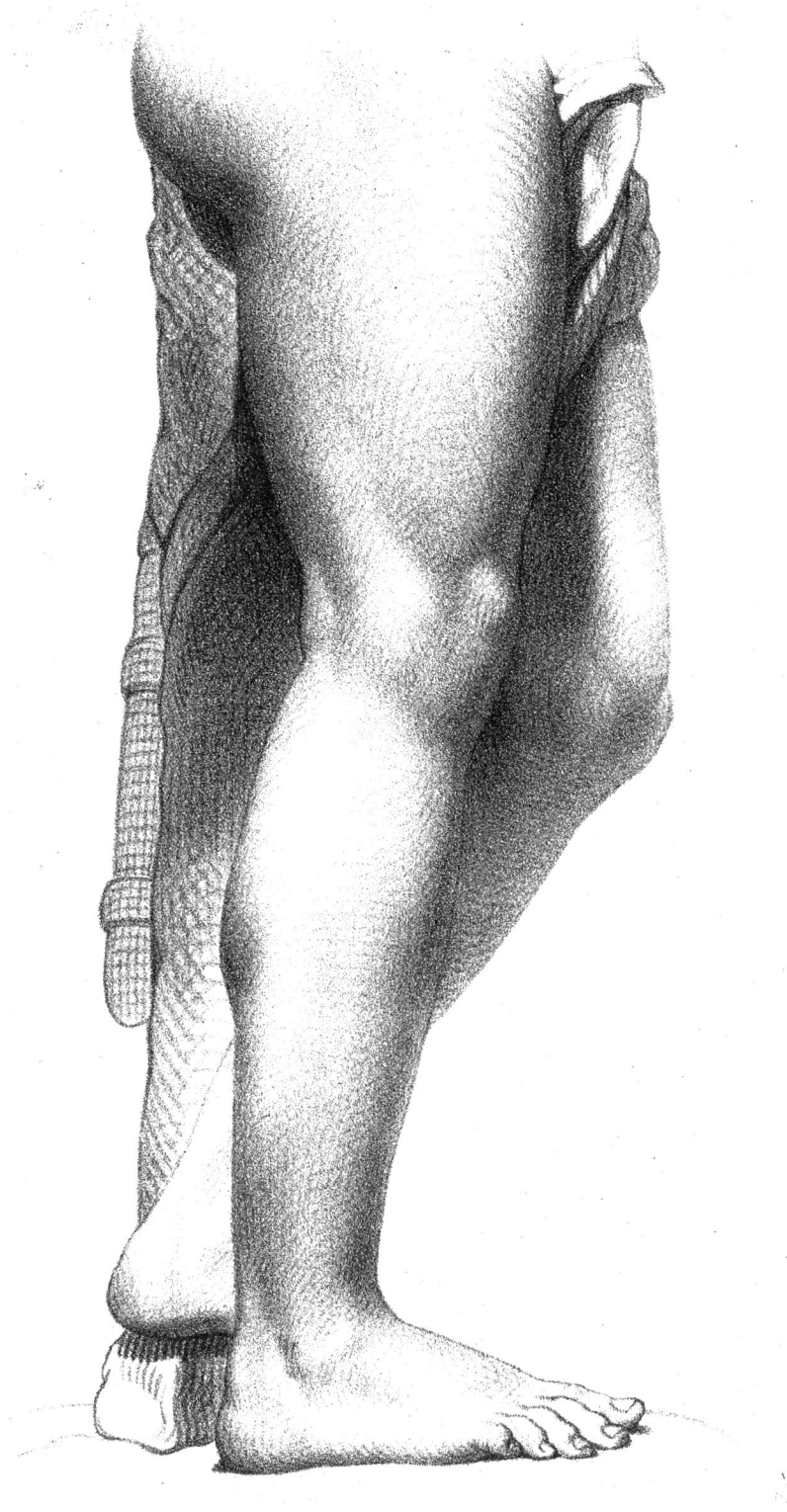

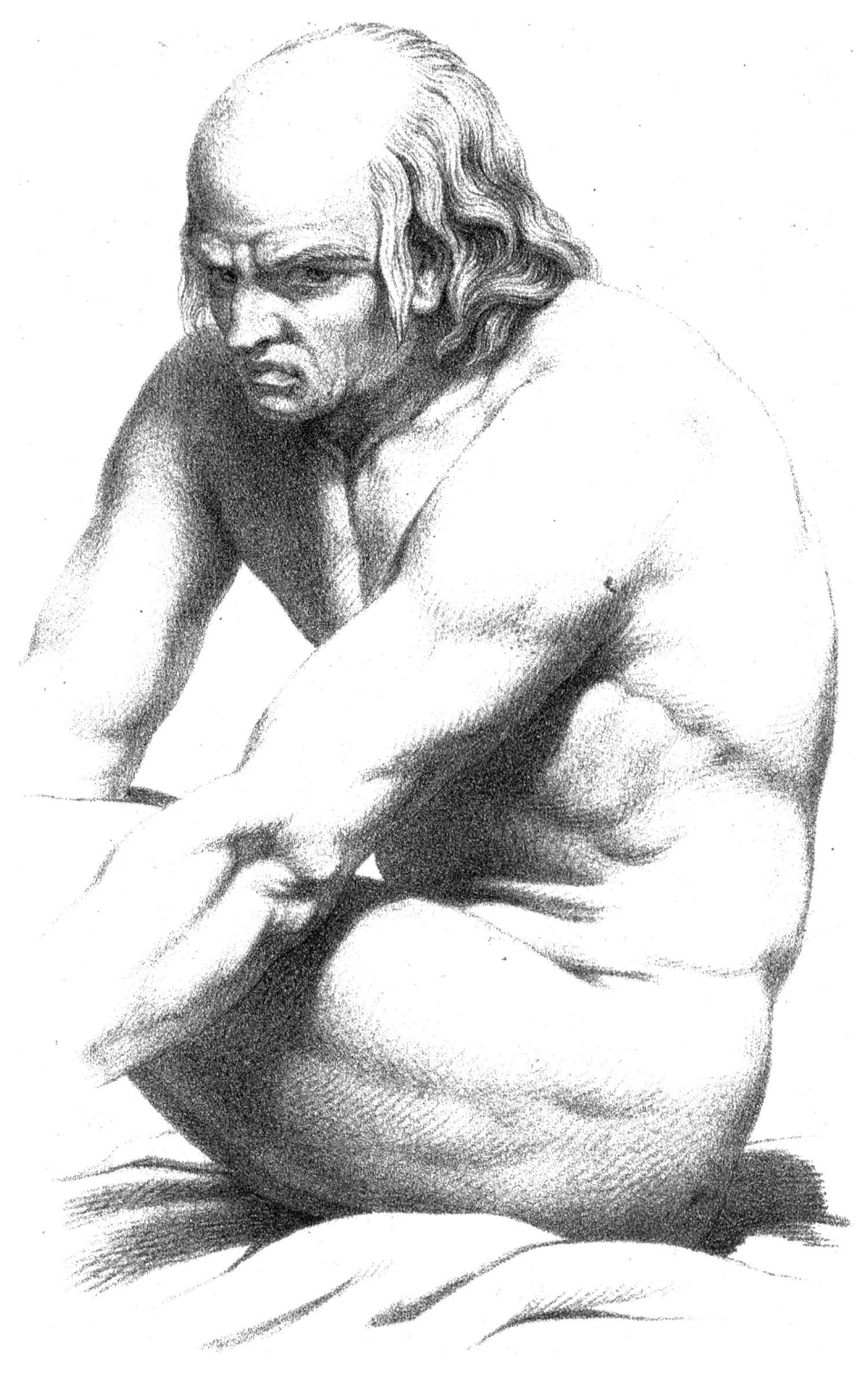

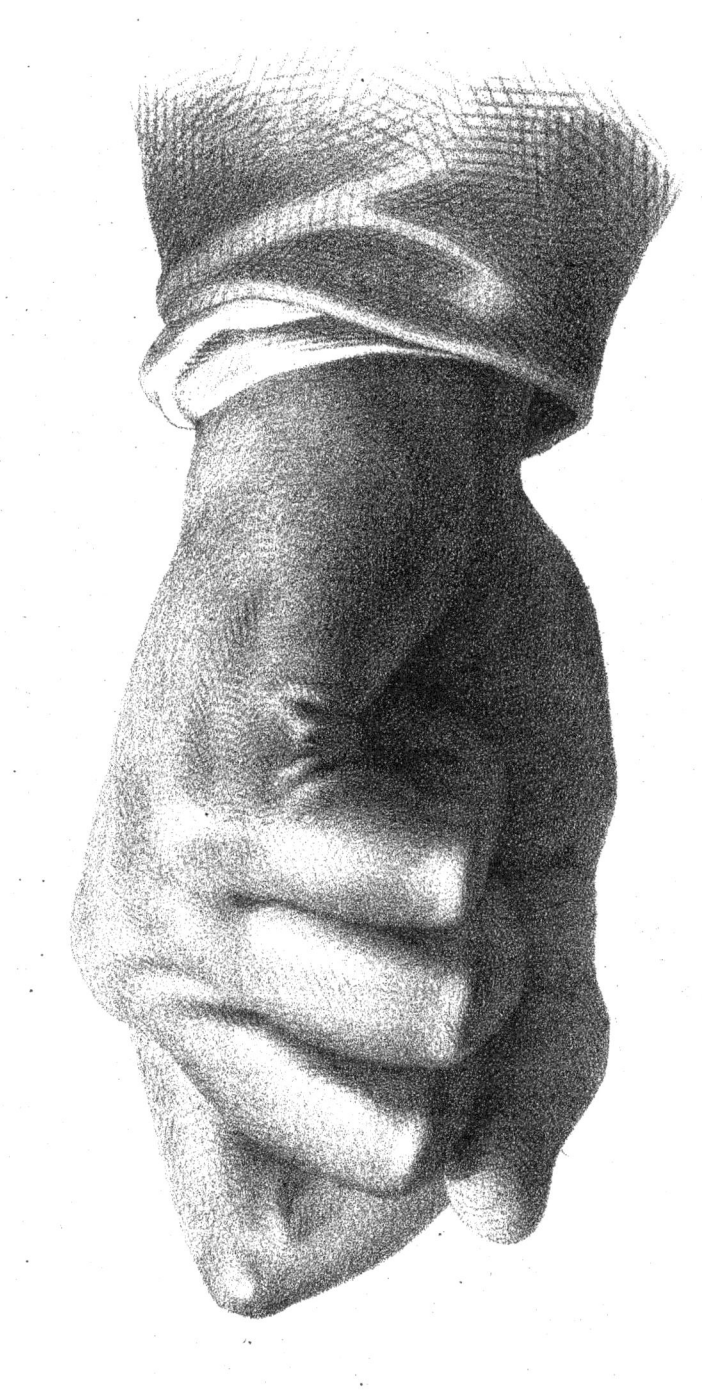

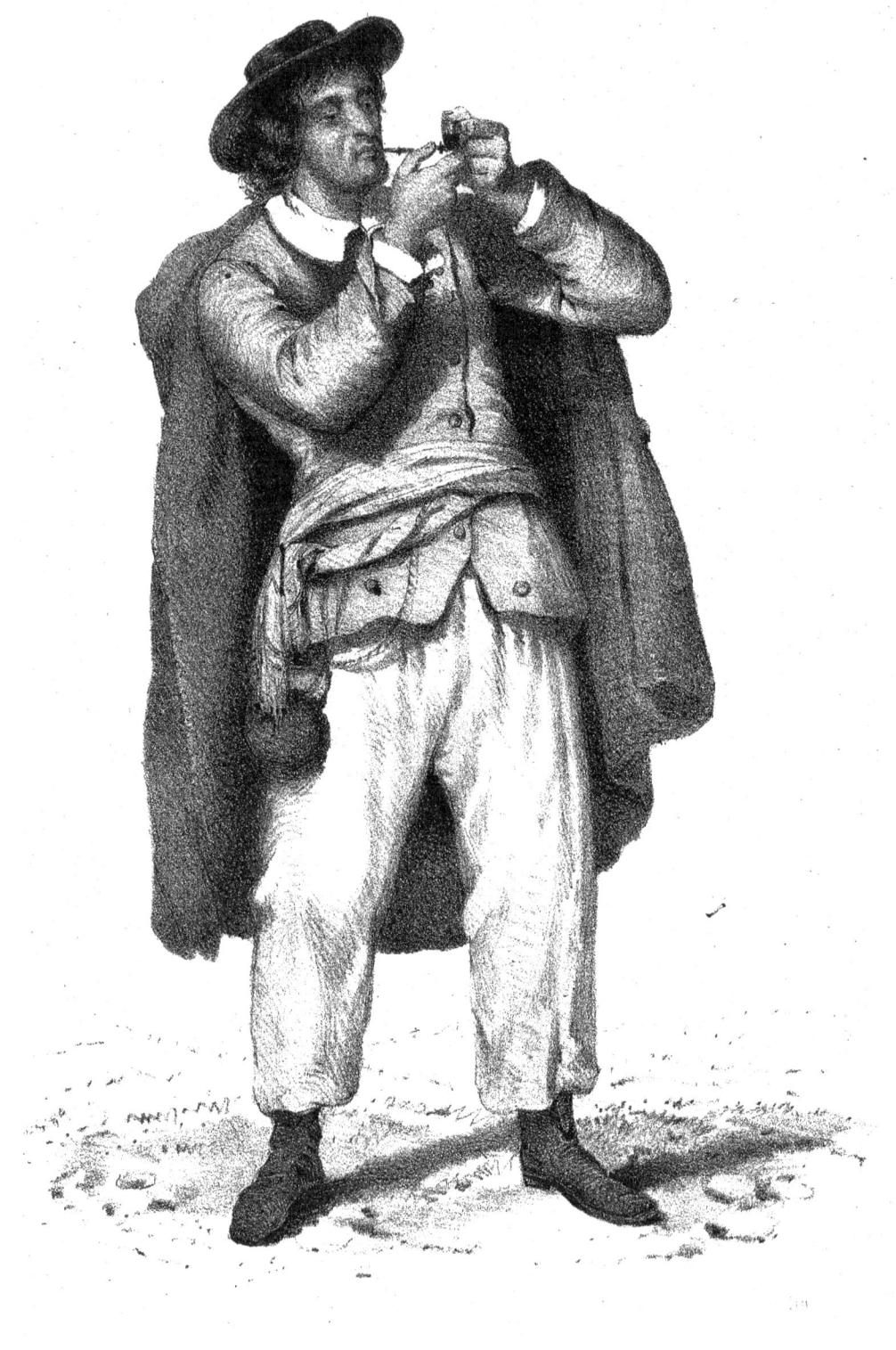

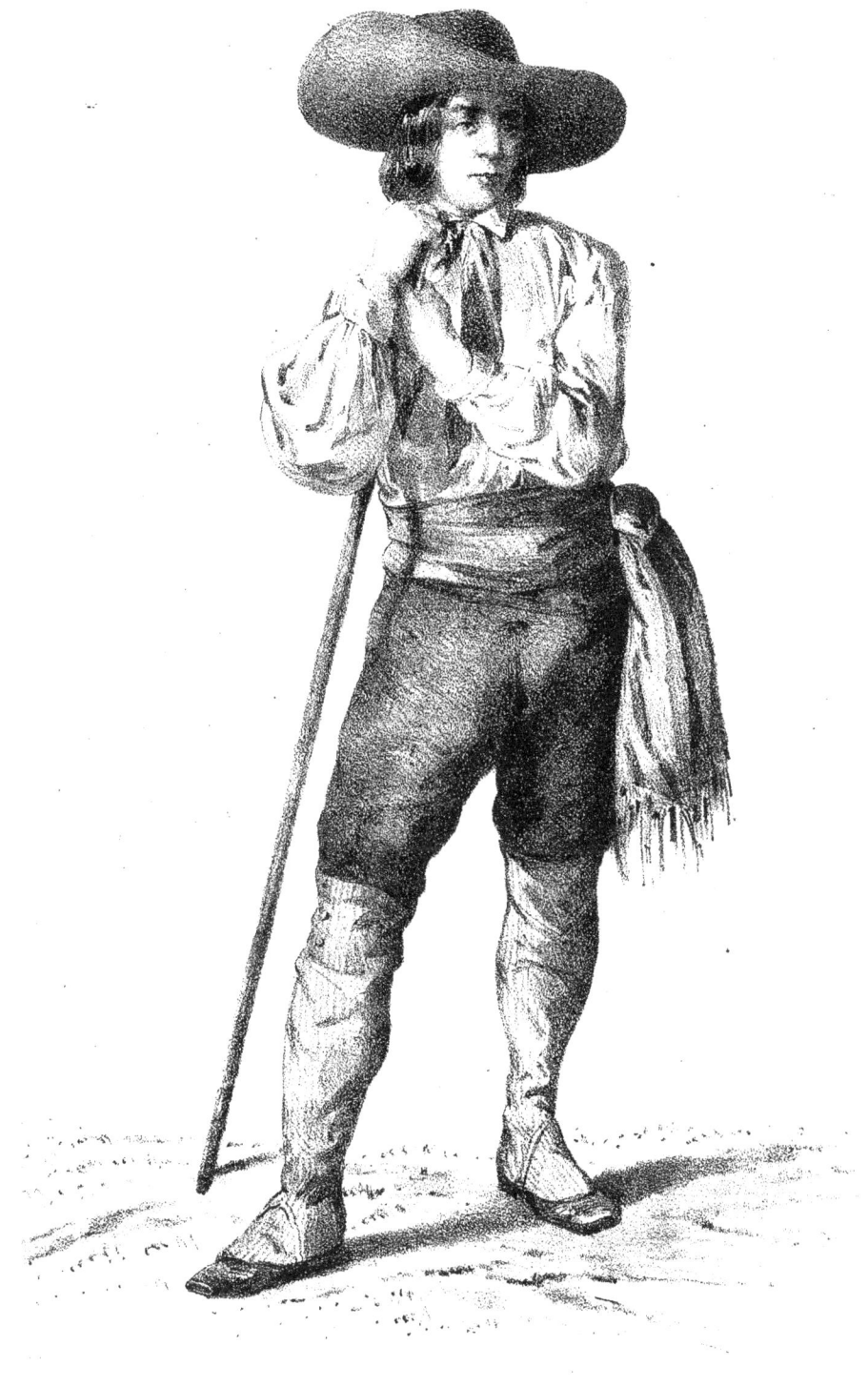

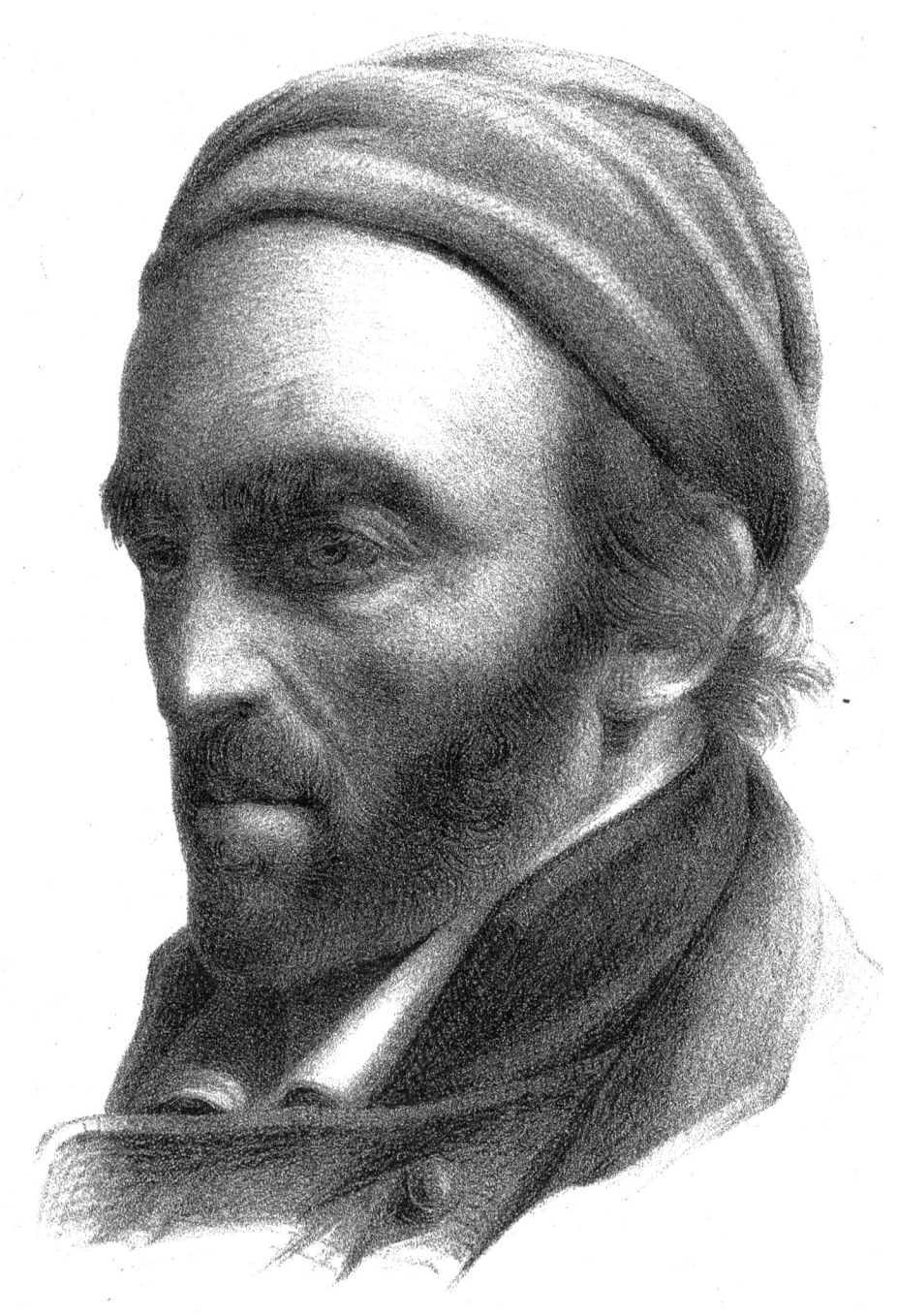

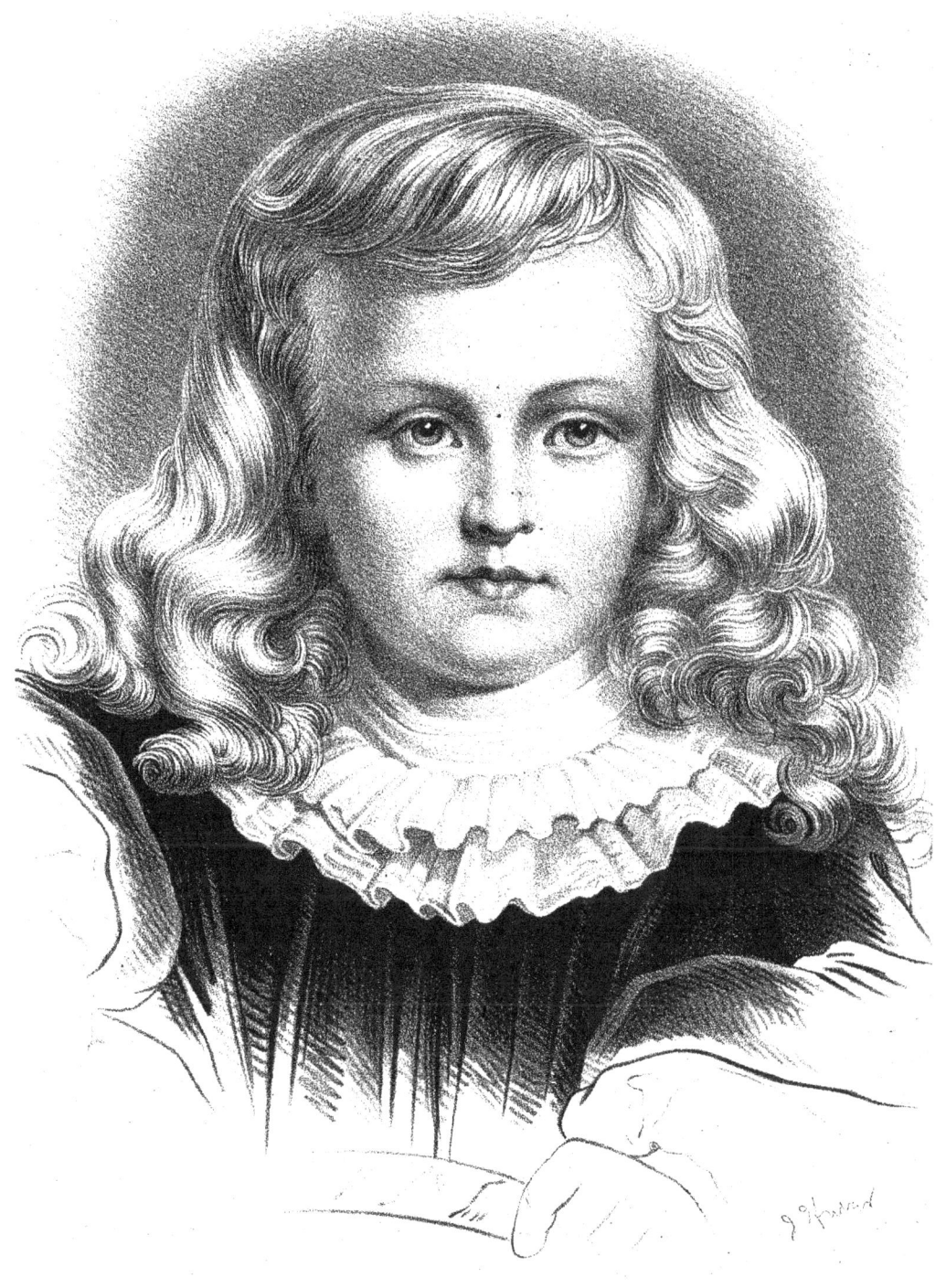

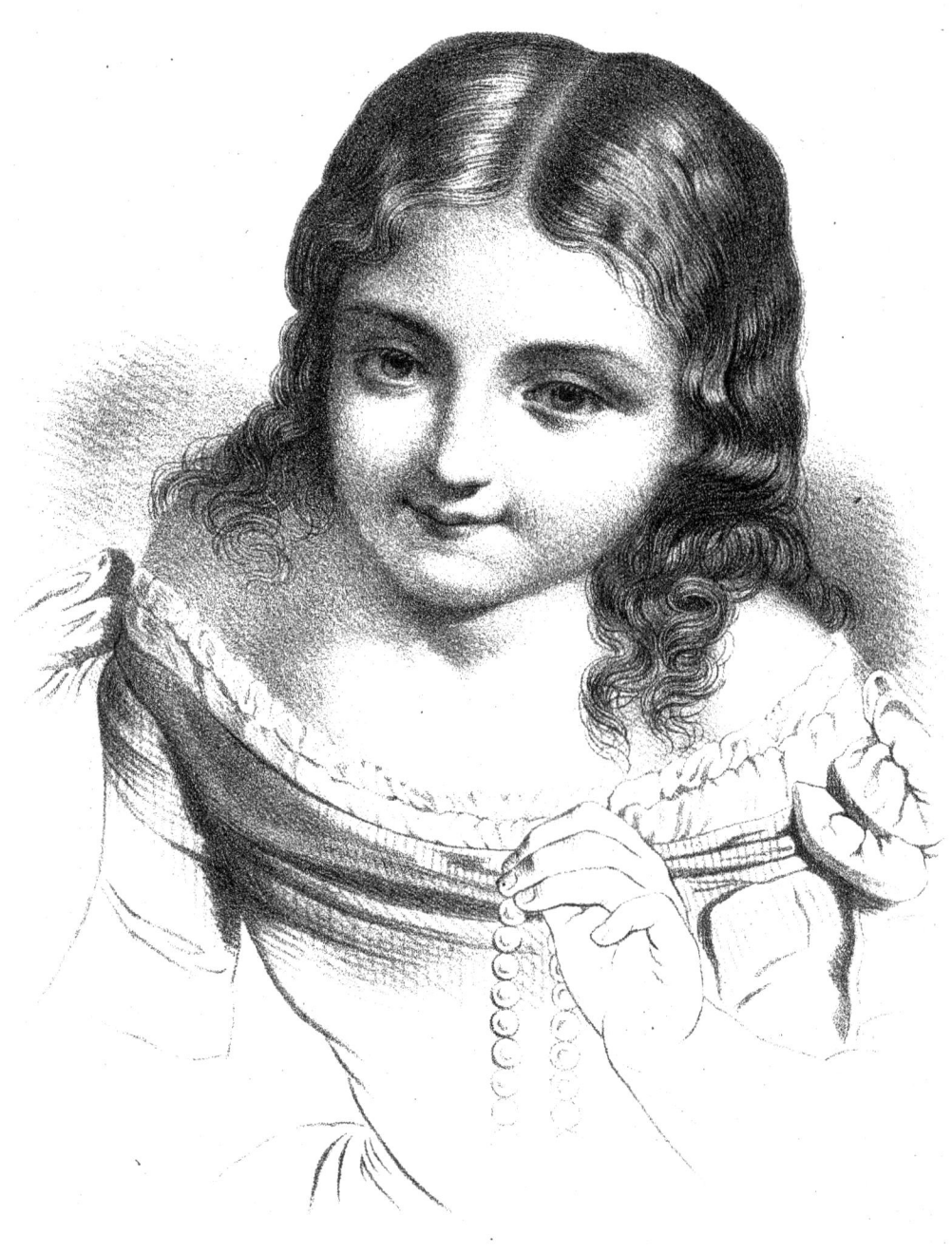

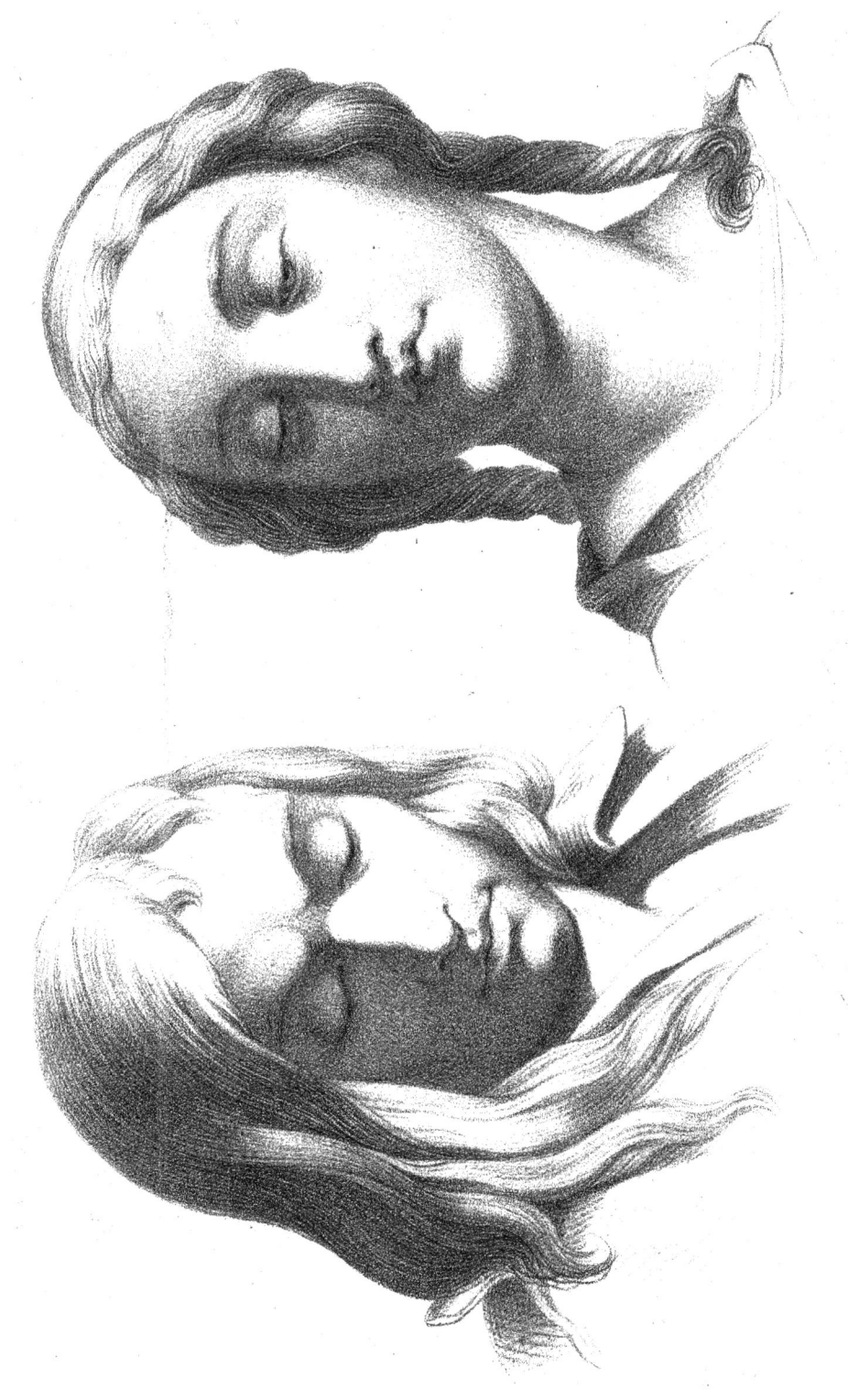

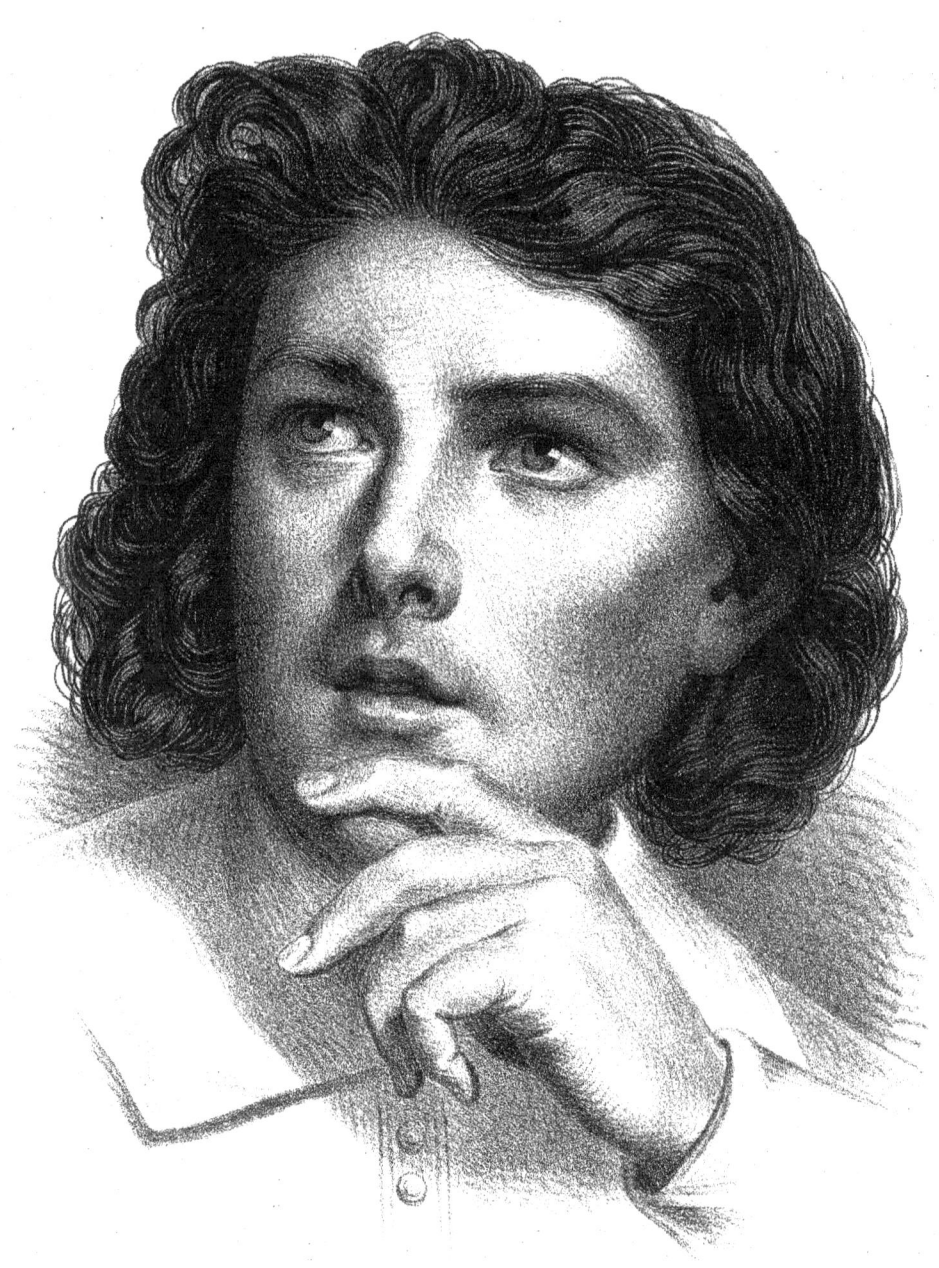

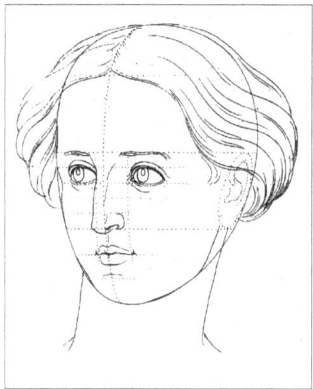

The Human Head
by Prof. Louis Bail
edited by Tom Richardson
ISBN 978-0982167830

How to draw the human head by the pre-eminent advocate for the teaching of drawing in schools in the mid nineteenth century, the inventor of the system of drawing used by many schools of the time.

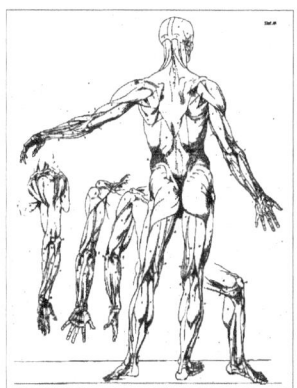

The Art Student's Guide
to the
Bones and Muscle of the Human Body:
and Lessons on Foreshortening
by Dr. Johann Gottfried Schadow
edited by Tom Richardson
ISBN 978-0982167823

This is a republished edition of Dr. Schadow's book which he designed for the benefit of his students at the Berlin Art Academy. It combines studies of anatomy based on his knowledge and the engravings of Bernhard Siegfried Albinus with three plates on human proportions plus detailed studies of the head tilted in different directions to demonstrate the effects of foreshortening

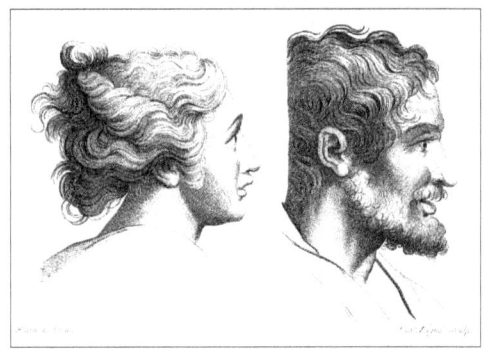

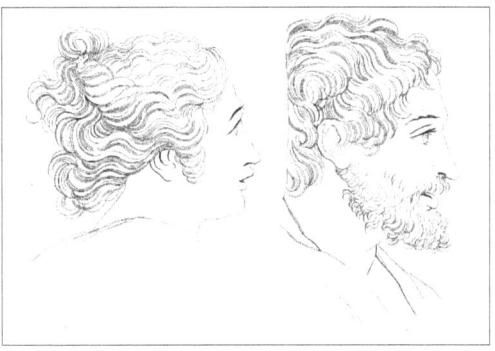

The School of Raphael
or the
Student's Guide to Expression in Historical Painting
by Louis Dorigny
described and explained by Benjamin Ralph
edited by Tom Richardson
ISBN 978-0982167849

These prints of the human head, showing the range of emotions and
expressions, were engraved by the most skilled artists of the day from
tracings and drawings made by Nicholas Dorigny from the famous cartoons
that Raphael designed in the early 1500s to be made into tapestries for the
Sistine Chapel. They were made into this book in 1859. Each plate has two
versions, the first a fully rendered, shaded print, the second an outline
version, with dotted lines showing where highlights and shadows will be
placed.

www.ingramcontent.com/pod-product-compliance
Lightning Source LLC
Chambersburg PA
CBHW080945170526
45158CB00008B/2375